With best wishes from
Mr. Houghton,-
Christmas 1993.

———

D1338618

A GUIDE TO THE BRITISH CATHEDRALS

GLOUCESTER CATHEDRAL

Photograph by Jones, Gloucester

A GUIDE TO THE
BRITISH CATHEDRALS

BY
LEIGHTON HOUGHTON

JOHN BAKER : LONDON

FIRST PUBLISHED 1973

JOHN BAKER: A. AND C. BLACK LTD
4, 5 AND 6 SOHO SQUARE LONDON W.I

ISBN 0 212 97007 0

PRINTED IN GREAT BRITAIN BY
BUTLER AND TANNER LTD, FROME AND LONDON

CONTENTS

Part I

Part II

I. WHAT IS A CATHEDRAL?

The pagan temple, in most instances, was regarded as the dwelling place of the god. In ancient Greece it consisted of a small, dark *cella* surrounded by a colonnaded verandah. In contrast, the Christian church is a place of assembly, designed for congregational worship.

The word church is derived from the Greek *kurikon*, meaning 'belonging to the Lord'. It is applied both to the community of those who worship and also to the building where they assemble. A church building is essentially a shelter for an altar, the table about which the congregation gathers for the celebration of the Lord's Supper.

Once the Christian Church became organized and settled the territories which it served were divided into dioceses, a name derived from the Greek word meaning 'inhabited place'. Each diocese is in the charge of a bishop and is known as the bishop's see from the Latin *sedes*, seat.

With the formation of a diocese a church was built, or an existing church adapted, to house the bishop's throne or *cathedra*. This was the cathedral church. A cathedral is, therefore, the principal church of a diocese sheltering the bishop's throne. It differs also from the parish church by having attached to it a Chapter House where the bishop may meet the clergy of the cathedral for the conduct of business.

In the sixth century a Church Council had forbidden the bishop's throne to be set up in a monastic church, but in this country the ruling was often ignored, so that our cathedral foundations are of three types:

Secular cathedrals, served by a Dean and Canons.

Monastic cathedrals, served originally by a Prior and community of monks.

New foundations, being generally existing parish churches

adapted as cathedrals on the formation of a new diocese, served by Dean or Provost and Canons.

In 1075 a Council of London decreed that the cathedral should always be situated in one of the larger towns of the diocese. In many cases a vast and elaborate building was erected over a period of years in response to civic pride. The cathedral of Salisbury, three times rebuilt, was on each occasion greatly enlarged: the eleventh-century church of Old Sarum was 173 ft. long and was enlarged in the following century to 316 ft., while the third building, erected on the new and present site in 1220, is 473 ft. in length. In France, the cathedral of Amiens on its completion was of sufficient size to hold the entire population of the town.

The earliest conception of a cathedral was that it should form a mission centre from which the bishop and his company of clergy might evangelize and minister to the diocese.

In the Middle Ages the cathedral was most probably the only commodious public building in the town. Its nave was considered by the people to be public property and was treated as a civic centre, even as a market-place and a hiring ground for labourers, while it served, too, as a meeting-place for the craftsmen's guilds which frequently supported their own chapel within it.

The monks, however, tended to regard the monastic cathedrals as their own property and discouraged their public use, in some cases even resisting the visitation of the bishop. But the monastic community served the locality by providing education and medical treatment, and shelter for the traveller and the homeless.

In the twentieth century the cathedral provides the focal point of the diocese, uniting the parishes in the provision of services for special occasions and particular groups, and maintaining a high standard of choral and musical accompaniment in its public worship.

II. THE CATHEDRAL OFFICERS

The office of bishop dates from the earliest days of the Christian Church. The title, meaning 'overseer', appears in the Epistles of the New Testament, though it was probably not until the third century that the office was established in its present form.

In the first century the bishop was the leader of a local congregation. Clement, Bishop of Rome at the close of the first century, greatly enhanced the office by claiming that every bishop received consecration in direct succession from the Apostles. When the Church became established and settled a specified territory was placed in the charge of the bishop and was known as his diocese.

There were at least three bishops in England as early as 314 when they are recorded to have attended a council on the Continent; when Pope Gregory sent Augustine to Kent in 597 he ordered him to contact the British bishops and present himself to them as their archbishop. Seven British bishops are said to have attended the conference, but they rejected his claims because of the haughtiness of his demeanour.

Augustine, however, was established as archbishop, with his cathedral at Canterbury; and other bishoprics were founded at Rochester (604) and York (625). The proposed bishopric of London failed to materialize owing to the hostility of the people, but Lichfield, Hereford, Winchester and Worcester were established during that century.

In Saxon times the establishment of a bishopric was dependent on the goodwill of the local king or chieftain, and the bishop's diocese was co-terminous with the local kingdom. While a number of cathedral churches were built during that period few relics of these remain, for the Normans despised their crude architecture and demolished them.

The fifteen bishoprics of Norman times continued

unchanged until the Reformation. Since these bishops were men of education and culture serving a largely illiterate population, it was natural that they should exercise considerable influence in matters of State and provide many of the monarch's most intimate advisers. Their choice was, therefore, a matter of concern to both king and pope and was normally the result of mutual agreement. Consequently the bishop was often more statesman than father-in-God, living in princely style and rarely visiting his diocese at all or having contact with his clergy.

'They were called bishops, but they were given up to pomp and display; they so devoted themselves to a military life and the world's pomp, that when they came to court all men marvelled at them for the crowd of men-at-arms who attended them.' So writes the author of the *Gesta Stephani* of the Bishops of Ely and Lincoln in the twelfth century.

At the dissolution of the monasteries Henry VIII created six new bishoprics, with monastic churches as their cathedrals, and episcopal appointments became solely a royal prerogative.

The medieval bishop necessarily spent much of his time in travel, journeying arduously over primitive roads throughout his far-flung diocese, supervising both the parish churches and the episcopal properties. In the early centuries it had been the task of the chief of his attendant deacons to keep the diocesan property in repair. The archdeacon, now normally in priest's orders, filled this office. Other clergy, known as canons, were attached to his cathedral under the jurisdiction of the dean.

The dean of a cathedral is next in rank to the bishop, of whom he is largely independent in the organization of the cathedral and its services, with responsibility for its maintenance. The appointment of a dean, as of a bishop, is made by the crown. Some of the new cathedrals, serving also as parish churches, have instead of a dean a provost with parochial responsibilities.

The earliest cathedrals were all administered by the canons under the dean; they were 'secular' clergy who were obedient to a common rule of life, the title canon meaning rule. Sometimes they were provided with dormitory and dining-room and each enjoyed the income of a farm or other property, from which is derived the title prebend, meaning provision.

The canons were responsible for the conduct of the cathedral services, some having particular duties: the precentor was in charge of music, assisted by the succentor; the chancellor, as keeper of the seal, acted as secretary and sometimes as master of the cathedral school; the treasurer was responsible for finance.

Latterly the canons tended to become as indolent and worldly as their bishops, more frequently absent from than present at their cathedral, some of them 'seeing the cathedral but once in their lives'. In consequence in the twelfth century the office of vicar-choral was initiated, each canon being responsible for paying a vicar-choral to occupy his place in choir and sing the services. Sometimes the vicars-choral, who may be likened to the professional choirman, were disciplined by a rule and provided with house and common room. They were liable to be suspended from office were they found to be 'talkative, hawkers . . . tavern-haunters or public players with dice'.

In several instances the Norman bishops ejected the secular canons and replaced them by monks. The majority of monastic cathedrals were in the charge of Benedictines. St. Benedict lived in the sixth century in Italy. The son of wealthy parents, he attempted to escape from the world by living as a hermit near Rome. Joined by admirers, he formed his monks into 'families' of twelve, each in the charge of an abbot (father) and bound by a rule of worship, work and study which became the pattern of all future monastic rules. From his monastery on Monte Cassino the Order spread rapidly throughout the west.

Other cathedrals were in the charge of Augustinian canons,

a preaching Order obedient to the Rule of St. Augustine founded in France in the eleventh century.

On the dissolution of the monasteries, completed by Henry VIII in 1539, the cathedrals were returned to the care of secular canons, and in every case—with the sole exception of Canterbury—the monastic prior became the dean and many of the monks became canons.

The Chapter House, an essential feature of the cathedral church, derives its name from the room where the monastic community met each morning to hear the reading of a chapter of the Benedictine Rule. The administrative body consisting of dean and canons is known as the chapter.

In the monastic community the cellarer was in charge of the kitchens, the sacrist in charge of church vestments, the almoner controlled the dispensation of charity, the hostiliar presided over the guest-house and the refectorer was in charge of the dining-room.

In addition to these officers there were also chantry priests. Wealthy donors would bequeath a sum of money to a cathedral or church for the support of a priest whose duty it was to chant a daily mass for the donor's soul; often the bequest also included the establishment of a chantry chapel. Although the chantry priest was supposed to engage in other work besides the recitation of his daily mass, he was popularly reputed to be indolent and latterly his office was held in disrepute.

III. THE CATHEDRAL BUILDERS

Although it was recorded of Gloucester Cathedral in 1242 that building had been carried out 'by the vigorous hands of the monks who resided on the spot' this was a quite exceptional happening, for the popular impression that our great cathedrals were erected as a kind of spare-time activity by untrained members of monastic communities is entirely false. In some instances the monks may have acted as additional labourers, but this was certainly a rare occurrence.

The bishop or a member of the cathedral chapter, monk or canon, initiated the building activity by the suggestion that such a work should be done, and on occasions acted as a kind of clerk of works, but the actual tasks of planning and building, the decisions as to design and sculptured ornamentations, were under the immediate supervision of the master-mason (*magister cementariorum*) and were accomplished by professional craftsmen engaged by him.

These master-masons travelled widely, sometimes remaining on the site throughout the weeks of building, sometimes—particularly in the latter half of the Middle Ages—paying frequent visits much as a modern architect might do. William of Colchester travelled to York to supervise the erection of the minster's great central tower, and rioting broke out in protest against the employment of an outsider. Henry Yevele, who was mason to the king, was employed both at Westminster Abbey and at Canterbury, and in his travels was influential in popularizing the Perpendicular style. The continental chevet-design of Canterbury's eastern limb is owed to the French mason, William of Sens, while both Wells and Gloucester are indebted to the same Somerset sculptors.

These masons were highly skilled, widely experienced and well paid, often travelling throughout Europe, working on commission. Robert, who worked at St. Alban's Abbey in 1077, 'excelled all the masons of his time' and was rewarded with the gift of a manor, which caused dissension among the monks, though Robert bequeathed it to the abbey on his death.

The masons who worked under the master's direction were of two classes: the freemasons who were skilled in the handling of freestone, shaping and carving it with marvellous ability, were the more highly paid; the rough-hewers were responsible for the more prosaic task of shaping the stone; but the status of both was raised after the epidemic of the

Black Death owing to the shortage of labour which resulted.

There were, of course, other craftsmen, often working in makeshift 'lodges' erected against the cathedral wall: the carpenter, both carving the furnishings and responsible for scaffolding; the smith working in wrought iron and caring for the masons' tools; the glazier devising his jewelled windows to fit the intricate stone tracery, though latterly demanding that the tracery be made to match his own designs.

All these craftsmen with their varied skills worked together as a disciplined team, even though individually under contract to the master-mason. Supporting them was unskilled labour hired locally. There were occasions when work was delayed by a strike, or outbreak of violence or the theft of materials.

The cost of building a cathedral, even though it was accomplished gradually over a long period of years, was enormous, and in more than one instance lack of funds called a halt to a project before its completion.

The money might be raised in a variety of ways: very occasionally there was a grant from the sovereign or payment by a wealthy patron, and considerable income was realized from bequests made on condition that periodical masses were offered for the donor's soul. A bishop or a chapter of canons might forfeit a portion of their stipends—not always willingly on the canons' part, or an appeal might be made, as when one of the monks of Durham was sent on a begging tour bearing a fragment of St. Cuthbert's robe. Indulgences were frequently offered for sale, purporting to free the purchaser from a period of purgatory after death; at Exeter a scribe was engaged in 1349 to write out eight hundred indulgences.

But the greatest revenue was realized by those who were so fortunate as to possess the shrine of a miracle-working saint. Then the offerings of multitudes of pilgrims were assured. If no authentic saint was available efforts would be made to provide one. At Rochester a murdered pilgrim who

had stayed but a night en route for Becket's shrine became
St. William, and the body of Edward II, entombed at
Gloucester when none other dared receive it, brought sufficient revenue to allow the whole church to be marvellously
re-sculptured in the Perpendicular style despite the fact
that the murdered king had, in life, been an indolent pleasure-
seeker and an incompetent weakling whose unworthy
favourites had brought the country to the verge of ruin.
Yet was ever money raised for nobler purpose or fruitful
in more splendid achievement?

IV. THE DEVELOPMENT OF THE CATHEDRAL BUILDING

In the earliest centuries the Christian communities were
scattered and small in number. They had neither the need nor
the resources to build places of worship; a room in a private
house was all that was required. In two of Paul's letters he
speaks of the church which is in the house of Prisca and
Aquila.

In the fourth century the Roman emperor recognized
Christianity as the official religion of the empire, the number
of Christians rapidly increased and there arose the necessity
to provide adequate meeting-places for worship. The emperor
himself built several churches to mark the holy places.

In designing the earliest churches the Christians were in-
fluenced by the design of the basilica where the magistrate
held his court and also possibly by that of the middle-class
house. The basilica was a simple rectangular building,
columns supporting the beam or entablature which upheld
its flat, wooden ceiling and allowing for aisles with lean-to
roofs, one or both ends of the building being apsidal, that
is, forming a bay. In the town basilica the apse was sometimes
separated from the body of the room by a screen, forming an

office where the magistrate had his chair flanked by the benches of his clerks. Such screens were called *cancelli*, from which is derived the word chancel.

Basically the entrance courtyard of the better-class Roman home was similarly planned, except that the courtyard itself was open to the sky. The colonnaded walks which flanked the courtyard would suggest the aisles and the *tablinum*, facing the entrance and sheltering the family table, successor of the sacred hearth, the sanctuary and altar.

The body of the church building is termed the nave, from the Greek *naos*, meaning temple, while the word aisle is derived from the Latin *ala*, a wing. In the earliest times the baptistry was a separate building.

Within the church the bishop's cathedra would occupy the eastern apse so that he faced the congregation across the holy table, presiding at the Lord's Supper, his attendant priests and deacons either side of him; in similar fashion the Jewish ruler of the synagogue sat facing the people, supported by the elders, and the Roman magistrate with his clerks. From this arrangement there originated the still prevalent but archaic practice of the priest celebrating the Communion with his back to the people: originally he was facing the bishop.

When Augustine built the first cathedral at Canterbury in 597, placing it in the charge of secular canons, it consisted of a simple, rectangular room with apses at either end, that at the east holding the altar and that at the west the cathedra.

The origin of the east–west orientation of the Christian church, with the people facing east, is of ancient, but doubtful derivation. The explanation that the congregation is reminded by the rising sun of Christ's second coming is without foundation; more probably it was a concession to pagan sun worship. When the Romans occupied Britain they adopted the Celtic god Sul, the sun-god, among other native deities, and at Bath erected a temple to his honour, coupling his name with that of Minerva.

The entrance to the early Christian churches was sheltered by a porch, as was the entrance to a Jewish synagogue. Since it became customary for those preparing for baptism to occupy the porch during worship it soon developed into a vestibule or narthex. But, with the introduction of infant baptism, the narthex gave way once more to the porch.

During the early centuries many Christians had died in persecutions and their graves had often been remembered and revered. Now, with the toleration of the faith, churches were sometimes erected over their graves and dedicated by name to the martyr. This was the origin of the crypt—from the Greek *kruptos*, meaning hidden—which was normally beneath the sanctuary. Crypts were subsequently used for the burial of leading Christians, such as the bishop, and to hold the local shrine or relics of the saints. As pilgrimages to such shrines grew in popularity it became necessary to move them to a more accessible position—generally behind the main altar; an ambulatory was then built through which pilgrims might walk to visit the shrine without disturbing the services at the altar, and the cathedra was moved to the south side of the sanctuary. Only one English cathedral, Norwich, has its cathedra in the original position, east of the altar.

The building was further enlarged by placing galleries above the aisles, with triple-arched openings providing a view of the nave and sanctuary, giving to the gallery the name triforium from the Latin *tri-fores*, triple doors. Such galleries were at one time used for the accommodation of women when, following the Jewish custom, they were seated apart from the men. The wall above the triforium was pierced by windows for the lighting of the nave and was called the clerestory.

Subsequent enlargements included the addition of transepts north and south for the accommodation of greater congregations and for the addition of more altars. Thus the building obtained the shape of a Latin cross. Towers were

B

erected for the hanging of bells and were often free-standing, as is the ancient bell-tower at Chichester.

V. THE PARTS OF A CATHEDRAL

The following descriptions are arranged in the order in which a visitor would normally encounter them.

TOWER. A cathedral may have one or many towers, or no tower at all. It may be situated at the western end, flanking the main entrance, or centrally at the meeting of nave, chancel and transepts. In the earliest centuries the tower was built to house bells, but it is often of structural importance, receiving the thrust of terminating vaults; sometimes it also had a defensive purpose. A tower which is free-standing, apart from the cathedral, is often referred to as a campanile.

STEEPLE. The steeple rarely has any functional purpose, but is an exuberant decoration, pointing to heaven. Gothic towers were frequently crowned by wooden steeples. Only one English cathedral, Lichfield, retains its original steeples on all three of its towers.

DOME. Domes are a characteristic of Byzantine and Renaissance architecture, roofing the central portion of the building, and semi-domes crowning the terminal apses of the church's limbs. In earliest centuries they were constructed of bricks and cement, or carved from solid rock, or built of light earthenware amphorae, their exterior protected by tiles or metal. While the Renaissance architects copied the Byzantine dome, they constructed it on the Gothic principle of ribs and light in-filling, covering it with a second, purely decorative dome, often curiously shaped and embellished with paint and gilding.

PORCH. There may be one or more entrance porches at the west end of the church, or these may be placed in the north or south walls, or attached to the transepts. The porch of the Gothic cathedral is often cavernous and richly decorated with statuary. It was used in medieval times for the opening portion of both baptism and marriage services, and on occasions for business meetings. The western porch was sometimes known as the Galilee, probably because processions concluded there, symbolizing our Lord's return to Galilee after his crucifixion at Jerusalem, of which the high altar was a reminder.

NARTHEX. A vestibule at the west end of a cathedral occasionally continuing round the north and south sides. It was occupied during services by those preparing for baptism and by those undergoing penance.

NAVE. The central portion of the church separated from the choir and sanctuary by a screen or pulpitum or both. In medieval times the nave was frequently used for secular purposes—meetings, plays, even market-stalls and dances. But its proper purpose was to serve as a processional way. Since the Reformation the nave has been used for the seating of the congregation as in a parish church.

AISLES. Lateral divisions of the body of the church, flanking the nave and sometimes also the choir and transepts. The aisle provided access to the side chapels which might be formed by the internal projection of buttresses.

TRIFORIUM. A gallery above the aisle, generally, but not invariably, without windows. In the early centuries it was allocated to the women of the congregation; occasionally it was used to accommodate additional altars.

CLERESTORY. The upper portion of the wall above the triforium, pierced by windows for the lighting of the nave.

TRANSEPTS. Extensions north and south at the crossing. Some cathedrals have additional transepts flanking the choir.

ROOD SCREEN. Screen placed between the western columns of the crossing. Normally it was used to support a crucifix or rood, with figures of St. Mary and St. John. In cathedrals where the public were permitted to worship in the nave it formed a reredos to their altar. Sometimes it upheld a loft or gallery from which the Gospel was read at Communion, access being gained either by stairs cut in the flanking pier or by ladder.

PULPITUM. A screen of solid stone placed between the eastern piers of the crossing, giving privacy to the choir and sanctuary where the monks or canons assembled for their services. It might support an organ.

CHOIR. That portion of the church between nave and sanctuary occupied by the singers, generally situated at the crossing, but frequently identical with the chancel.

CHANCEL. Originally the space before the sanctuary which was railed off by low, waist-high screens called *cancelli*. In Byzantine churches the *cancelli* developed into a solid screen of full height, shutting the sanctuary from view, but pierced by doors which were opened for portions of the service. In the West the chancel became much enlarged in medieval times, accommodating the seats of canons, monks or vicars-choral. The removal of pulpitum and rood screen during times of religious upheaval, such as the Reformation, led to introduction of altar rails as a replacement.

PRESBYTERY. The area between choir and sanctuary, now often identical with the chancel, deriving its name from the Latin *presbyter*, priest, as accommodating the seats of the clergy.

SANCTUARY. The eastern portion of the church where the altar stands; from the Latin *sanctus*, holy.

RETROCHOIR. That part of the building which lay behind the sanctuary where it was customary to place the shrine.

AMBULATORY. A colonnaded passageway circling the rear of the sanctuary, giving access to the retrochoir or to eastern chapels. It was designed to allow the passage of pilgrims visiting the shrine and avoid disturbance of services at the high altar.

WATCHING CHAMBER. A balcony or room raised on a higher level and approached by a stair, from which watch might be kept on the precious stones and other valuables attached to the shrine. Only two watching chambers survive in English cathedrals, at Oxford and St. Albans. At Canterbury dogs were used to guard the shrine of Thomas à Becket.

LADY CHAPEL. A chapel dedicated to the Virgin Mary, most frequently dating from the thirteenth century when her veneration gained popularity; normally erected at the eastern extremity of the cathedral.

CHEVET. Three, five or more chapels grouped round an eastern apse and approached by an ambulatory. The chevet is a feature of French Gothic and its appearance in England, as at Canterbury, indicates the influence of a French master-mason.

CHANTRIES. Chapels erected within the cathedral by private donation to which is attached an endowment for the payment of a priest to 'chant' masses for the repose of the donor's soul. The chantry chapel often shelters the tomb of the donor, which may also form its altar.

TREASURY. A room within the cathedral used for the safe keeping of valuables, such as communion plate and flagons.

CRYPT. An underground chamber, normally beneath the chancel, used originally for burials or the display of relics; sometimes furnished with altars.

UNDERCROFT. Normally identical with the crypt, but occasionally a room on ground level situated beneath an upper room and used as a treasury, as at Wells.

BAPTISTRY. That part of the cathedral where the font is situated, normally—but not invariably—at the western end and adjacent to the main entrance in order that those entering the building may be reminded that by baptism they gained entry to the family of Christ. The baptistry floor may be on a lower level than that of the nave, symbolizing the belief that the baptized enters into the death and entombment of Christ that by God's grace they may rise to new life. When adult baptism was the norm the baptistry was most often a separate building, circular in design. In medieval times baptism was administered only three times a year—on the eve of Epiphany, and on Easter Day and Whitsunday. The water in the font, having been blessed, was retained and protected by a font cover which was locked in position.

CHAPTER HOUSE. A room adjacent to the cathedral used for business meetings of bishop or dean and canons.

CLOISTERS. A covered walk surrounding a quadrangle normally situated on the south side of the building as being the sunnier. Derived from the Latin *claustrum*, closed. In monasteries the cloisters gave access to the domestic rooms.

GARTH. A paddock or lawn enclosed by cloisters and often possessing a well.

CLOSE. The area enclosed by the houses of cathedral officers, dean and canons, within the cathedral precincts.

CONSISTORY COURT. A courtroom where the bishop or his chancellor presides over the hearing of such cases as involve episcopal jurisdiction. It may be situated within the cathedral church.

SACRISTY. A room set apart for the robing of the clergy and as a repository for their vestments.

VI. THE DEVELOPMENT OF CATHEDRAL ARCHITECTURE

The development of cathedral architecture has been a continuous evolution, beginning with the simplicity of the Roman style and reaching its greatest elaboration in this country in the splendour of the Perpendicular. It represents a seeking to solve the problem of weight and mass, to escape the appearance of solidity and to find a unity of design.

No cathedral illustrates a single style, though one style predominates in each. None of these great churches, with the sole exception of St. Paul's, was completed by the architect, or master-mason, who was responsible for its initial design. Remarkably, none of our cathedral churches evolving over five centuries, displays work of decadence, though on some of them the hand of the eighteenth-century restorer has fallen heavily and with ill effect.

James Wyatt, called by Pugin 'this pest of cathedral architecture', is chief among those who, particularly in the eighteenth century, have been judged to be responsible for more damage than all the iconoclastic Puritans and reformers who flourished before them. But our cathedrals remain, despite the wounds inflicted upon them by such as these, the country's richest treasure, memorials to the faith and genius of men who strove to materialize spiritual truth in stone and wood and coloured glass.

About the fifth century the Roman style developed gradually into the Romanesque, an architecture characterized by the round arch and the barrel or groined roof of which the curvation was formed in the mortar. The addition of transepts north and south, combined with the long nave and short eastern limb gave the church the design of a Latin cross. Basically the building was formed of a series of bays each consisting of arcade, triforium and clerestory, separated by massive piers and columns, rubble filled, and the small, deeply splayed windows admitted little light. This was an architecture of fear, of man's spirit imprisoned by the hostility of his neighbour and by his inability to control the materials with which he worked. Yet the Romanesque displayed latterly those features which were to characterize the Gothic style: the lancet window, the flying buttress and the pointed arch.

Meantime, in the East, the Christian architect was developing the Byzantine style, the Emperor Constantine having moved his throne to Byzantium, renaming it Constantinople, within a few years of his recognition of the faith.

Here the Christian builder was faced with a new problem: the almost total absence of wood. He therefore designed his church on the model of the Zoroastrian tomb—square, brick-built and roofed by a dome. The dome was supported by four massive piers bearing arches, the square thus formed being converted into a circle by joining the abutments of the arches with concave triangles of masonry called pendentives. Each of the four arches framed an arm of the building which terminated in an apse and was roofed by a barrel vault or a semi-dome, the apses sometimes formed in the thickness of the wall. The completed church presented the design of a Greek cross. Light was admitted by windows in the dome and, in some instances, by additional round-headed windows in the wall of the apses. Later builders raised the central dome on a drum which was pierced by windows. The outer surface of the dome was often protected by a tiled roof and sometimes by an outer, ornamental dome.

When in the eighth century the emperor forbade the making of religious images, craftsmen from the East flooded into Italy, and Byzantine architecture met with Romanesque, introducing modifications of both styles. In the East the Church, cut off by the Mohammedan invader, retained the Byzantine style practically unaltered, but in the West, as the communities of men became more settled and more confident of the future, they expressed their new freedom of spirit in the architectural style called Gothic, exchanging the darkness of the ponderous Romanesque building for an increasing lightness and delicacy of design. It need hardly be said that the term Gothic, applied as one of derision in the seventeenth century, is entirely misleading; the style owed nothing to the barbarous Goth. The builder sought now to make an illusion of weight, substituting for ponderous mass a delicate structural skeleton of ribs and buttresses, permitting walls to be replaced by vast areas of brilliantly coloured glass.

In England Gothic architecture found unity and perfection in the Perpendicular style, with the ethereal beauty of fan-vaulted roof upheld by slender columns. While on the continent the Gothic cathedral is characterized by its deeply recessed porches and the soaring height of nave and chancel, in this country its characteristics are the central tower and the square termination of the eastern limb, and height replaced by length.

In 1483, when Constantinople fell before the conquering armies of the Saracens, there was a further exodus of scholars and craftsmen to the West, bringing with them ancient manuscripts and forgotten skills. From this movement sprang the Renaissance, giving new inspiration to men who, stimulated by the rebellious preaching of such men as Wyclif and Luther, were searching for new freedoms of expression.

The architecture of the Renaissance looked back to that of ancient Greece, imperial Rome and the majesty of old Byzantium. It was essentially an architecture of individualism, of pride, and wealth, and jealous, arrogant patrons, and it gave birth to the professional architect.

In the seventeenth century the Counter-Reformation produced on the Continent the garish and opulent architecture of the Baroque, to be modified in the next century by the gentler spirit of Rococo. But neither style found favour in England where, in the eighteenth century, Neo-Classicism attempted to mirror exactly the ancient Grecian style. The nineteenth-century architect was for the most part content with an imitative Gothic. Today the imaginative use of new materials and techniques, of steel and reinforced concrete, has given to the twentieth century the opportunity for new vision and exciting experiment.

VII. THE ARCHITECTURAL STYLES

Very rarely does a single building exhibit a single style of architecture. In almost every case the original design has been modified by later additions and alterations, while between the passing of one style and the coming to birth of its successor there is a transitional period when characteristics of both styles appear together.

The following pages outline the main features of those styles to be found in the British cathedrals, but there are innumerable exceptions to the rules and it is often advisable to look for a combination of features rather than for one before attempting to date any portion of the building.

Each style held sway for approximately a century except Perpendicular Gothic which predominated for twice that time.

Romanesque or Norman:	1050–1150
Early English Gothic:	1150–1250
Decorated Gothic:	1250–1350
Perpendicular Gothic:	1350–1550
Renaissance:	17th century
Neo-Classicism:	18th century

ROMANESQUE OR NORMAN

GENERAL FEATURES

The design is that of a Latin cross, formed by transepts, and there are aisles or double aisles; occasionally double transepts are found. The nave is normally twice the width of the aisles and is separated from a short, rectangular chancel by an arch supported by corbels. Walls are massive, formed of small stones with thick mortar joints or rubble with ashlar facing. Normally there will be both triforium and clerestory, but sometimes the aisles rise to the full height of the nave. There may be chapels formed by the divisions of interior buttresses.

TOWER

There may be a central tower dividing nave and chancel or twin towers at the west end. The tower will be square, often rising only to the height of the nave ridge, strengthened by rudimentary buttresses called pilasters which reach only to the stringcourse of the first story.

ENTRANCE

The doorway is in the thickness of the wall, flanked by shafts in receding orders, with square moulding above. Sometimes there is a central column.

ROOF

The exterior ridge roof normally protects a barrel vault, with lean-to roofs over aisles. Late Romanesque exhibits groined roofs, sometimes with ribs, a traverse arch at the intersection of the diagonal ribs forming a sexpartite vault.

WINDOWS

Narrow, round-headed and splayed on the interior, either single or in groups. Shafted in the jambs. Wheel windows are found and occasionally tympanums pierced by windows. In towers the windows are confined to the upper stories, often increasing in number as the stories rise.

ARCHES AND COLUMNS

Massive piers, sometimes with attached half-columns, alternate with rubble-filled columns axe-carved with fluting, spirals, etc. Arches are round, without keystone, with receding, recessed soffits. Cushion capitals bear abacus and are sometimes chamfered. The plinth is square, carved at corners. Voussoirs may be moulded.

DECORATION

The arches of doorways exhibit ornate axe carving. Corbel tables formed of miniature round arches ornamented with masks and decorative carving. The carving of the tympanum is shallow, and shallow-carved figures of saints may occupy niches. Traces of paintwork in bold design may be found on columns or walls, or a crucifix painted on the face of a pier to act as reredos for a subsidiary altar. Capitals may be axe-carved, with scolloping, but sculpturing may be of later date. A wealth of characteristic mouldings include zigzag, chevron, pellet, beakhead, billet, double-cone, cable, scollop and nailhead, also diaper and outward-turned crocket. Interior walls are plain, being originally hung with tapestries.

The chisel, though known in Roman times, did not come into use until the end of the Romanesque period.

EARLY ENGLISH GOTHIC

GENERAL FEATURES

The design is of a Latin cross, with single or double transepts and chapel or chapels at the eastern termination. The bold buttresses have a projection equal to their width, gable heads or offsets, with pinnacles; they are sometimes chamfered. Flying buttresses may form a feature of the exterior instead of being hidden under the aisle roof as in late Romanesque. Parapets have open tracery and may form an exterior gallery at the west end. Aisles are single or double and the eastern end may have a polygon apse. Triforium and clerestory, the former often highly decorated, tend to be smaller than in Romanesque, their combined height being equal to that of the nave arcade. There may be a beautiful, but unrelated western façade, rich with sculpture, the figures being originally coloured against a gilded background.

TOWER

Central tower or, more rarely in this country, twin western towers. Broad spire. Pierced arcading.

ENTRANCE

Deep porch replacing narthex. Porches north and south. Doorways pointed and trefoil.

ROOF

More acute in pitch; lead-covered. Ribs on groins. Quadri- and sexpartite vaulting. Ridge rib appears at end of period.

WINDOWS

After 1230 the single lancet is replaced by twin lights with foliated head. West end has lancet windows in tiers on wheel window. Windows set in deep jambs, with hood mouldings. Divisions between lights become thinner. Plate and bar tracery, with added cusps.

ARCHES AND COLUMNS

All arches are pointed, with numerous detached shafts joined by mouldings. Piers are compound and columns slender. Arches of clerestory occasionally stilted. The abacus is shallower, square or round; octagonal towards close of period. Diaphragm arches. Foliated capitals, with foliage stemming from bell, the capital large and richly decorated.

DECORATION

Deep undercutting is characteristic of the sculpture. Figures are finely sculptured, with flowing drapery. The stringcourse is surmounted on blocks and corbel tables have trefoil arches; pinnacles are large. Niches are richly carved. Water-moulding is characteristic, i.e. a deep hollow between two round mouldings. Mouldings include dogtooth in deep recess, stiffstalk foliage, tooth, crocket, four-leaf, pyramid, roll and fillet.

DECORATED GOTHIC

GENERAL FEATURES

Latin cross. Buttresses are often paired and rise in stages, with offsets and gables; sometimes there are niches for statuary. The nave widens, and triforium and clerestory are smaller. Buttresses may have decorated pinnacles.

TOWER

Battlemented parapets and pinnacles. Richly carved cornices. Spires sometimes pierced by windows.

ENTRANCES

Doorways are less recessed, jambs more shallow, shafts attached. There may be rich carving, hood mouldings and a niche above the porch.

ROOF

Less steep. Moulded ribs and bosses. Lierne vaulting.

WINDOWS

These increase in size and include large rose windows. Hood mouldings. Mullions.

ARCHES AND COLUMNS

Compound piers, with engaged shafts cut from the same stone, the shafts having separate mouldings and their own capitals. Decorated soffits. Ogee and cinquefoiled arches.

DECORATION

Gargoyles and grotesque sculptures. Tracery is geometrical, curvical and flowing, pierced over doorways. Ornamentation depicts natural leaves, animal and human heads, but less deeply undercut. Cusps are cut from the same stone as the tracery. Foliage wreaths round the well of the capital and in hollows of dripstone and cornice. Ballflower and the inward curved crocket are characteristic of the period. Finials are richer and statues stand beneath ornate canopies, the niche itself ornamented with diaper.

PERPENDICULAR GOTHIC

GENERAL FEATURES

Latin cross. Buttresses increase in size, double at angles, diagonally placed at corners and sometimes half-arched. Flying buttresses are pierced. The triforium shrinks, sometimes replaced by ornamental panelling, and the clerestory windows are enlarged.

TOWER

Often embattled and with spire. Sometimes crocketted. Pinnacles are richly carved; there may be figures in niches, ornamentation increasing with the higher stories.

ENTRANCES

Depressed arch under square dripstone. Shafted jambs.

ROOF

Ornate fan-vaulting, stalactites and inverted cones. Richly carved openwork timber roofs; hammerbeam. The stone vault is now constructed on an exactly opposite principle to earlier periods. Instead of a skeleton of ribs carrying the weight and thrust, with light in-filling, the vaulting is now solid and the ribs decorative.

WINDOWS

Wide compared with height, thick central mullions, transoms and straight-line tracery. Sometimes there is a gallery in front of window. There may be double tracery.

ARCHES AND COLUMNS

Arches four-centred, less pointed. Piers are oblong, with moulded shafts rising to vaulting and carried round arch. Capitals tend to disappear.

DECORATION

Carving, depicting portcullis, rose, fleur-de-lys, trefoil and crocket, becomes more coarse. Corbel figures appear between windows and angels holding shields. Spandrels bear shields and foliage.

To this period belong chantry chapels, elaborate rood screens, canopied choir stalls, poppyhead ornament and misericords.

RENAISSANCE

GENERAL FEATURES

The design is that of a Greek cross, a symmetrical building having few, but large parts. Grecian columns bear entablature and pediment. Pilasters rise to decorative capitals. Each stage of the building is defined by a cornice. Lower walls are often rusticated.

TOWERS

Rare. Sometimes crowned by lantern.

ENTRANCES

Columned portico approached by wide steps. Doorways round-arched or square-headed, crowned by pediment; unrecessed.

ROOF

Dominated by ribbed dome on drum, sometimes crowned with lantern. The drum may be circled by a colonnaded gallery, supported within by piers and pendentives.

WINDOWS

Round or square-headed, with hood moulding, filled with plain glass.

ARCHES AND COLUMNS

Round arches without orders supported by piers or Grecian columns. Wide capitals with rectangular abacus ornately sculptured. Moulded, projecting cornices and richly decorated architraves.

DECORATION

Mosaic and frescoes. Volutes and acanthus. Coffered and boldly decorated soffits. Garlands and sensational statuary, naked and pagan. Terra-cotta. An elaborate baldacchino shelters the altar. Marble abounds. Candelabra.

Neo-Classical

GENERAL FEATURES

The building is rectangular, without transepts. The lower walls are rusticated, the roof has a balustrade. Ornamental pilasters and projecting cornices.

TOWER

Stories marked by cornices. Bears cupola on drum or lantern.

ENTRANCES

Square-headed and insignificant.

ROOF

Ridge roof, with coffered, plaster ceiling.

WINDOWS

Round-headed or circular; exterior rusticated.

ARCHES AND COLUMNS

Round arch supported by Grecian columns which rise from massive plinths to ornamental cornice.

DECORATION

White and gilded plaster.

VIII. A NOTE ON WOOD CARVING

THE THIRTEENTH-CENTURY doors were formed of two boards, the interior face horizontal, the outer vertical, ornamented with nails; porches with plain gables and uncarved bargeboard. Jamb and half-arch were cut from a single timber. Screens had shafts tenoned into head and dowelled to boards, with trefoiled and moulded arches. Latterly

c

spandrels were pierced and traceried. Stalls were plain, chests cut from a solid trunk or made of planks, dowelled, ornamented with stiff leaf foliage and scrollwork. Cupboards were formed in the thickness of wall or pier, with wooden doors.

THE FOURTEENTH CENTURY saw doors ornamented with ironwork, and later with applied tracery. The porch bargeboard was carved and roofs had thick, massive braces, and latterly traceried spandrels. Screens show slight projection of shafts and geometrical tracery. Stalls had elaborately carved bench ends, arcading and, latterly, canopied tabernacles. Misereres are finely carved, the carving confined in a rectangle and foliage bursting from stems. Effigies too are finely carved; tombs sometimes have cadavers.

THE FIFTEENTH-CENTURY doorways were of frame construction ornamented on the outer face, while hammerbeam roofs and screens had elaborate and delicate tracery, sometimes arched and vaulted and with lofts. Stalls had traceried panels and poppyhead finials, and desks had buttresses. Misericords bore long-stemmed foliage and semi-polygon carving. Heraldry, inscriptions and rebuses appear in carving, also the crocket and cusp.

THE SIXTEENTH CENTURY introduced linenfold panelling and flowing tracery, elaborately carved roofs with angel corbels, and lecterns having a canopied figure on their stem.

Normally the medieval woodcarver expected his work to be coloured; panels were left plain, ready for the painter; some of these paintings have been preserved.

IX. A NOTE ON STAINED GLASS

TWELFTH CENTURY

Pot metal glass was used; that is, glass and colouring were fused together. In early centuries this glass was inserted in small pieces in pierced marble window fillings and in plaster. Patterns were painted on the glass with brown paint which was then fired. The earlier the date of the glass the less it is painted. The various coloured pieces were leaded together and these pot metal windows were mosaics of deep and brilliant colour. Lettering was sometimes added by painting an area with brown paint and scratching out the letters with a sharp point. Windows were also made of 'white' glass (which actually had a greenish tint) and the pattern formed by the leading, dummy leads being sometimes added, being laid on the surface of a piece of glass, not as a joint. Small fragments of coloured glass were sometimes added to these white windows.

THIRTEENTH CENTURY

The colour is brilliant and the windows have narrow borders of colour. Lettering made in reverse by blocking out the surrounding area. Medallion pictures, with a background of cross-hatching, geometrical patterning and diapered spandrels. Figures are stiff, with widely splayed feet; the same drawing is sometimes used to represent different figures.

Grisaille glass came into use, grey in colour, painted with natural foliage, a separate leaf to each pane. Medallions have diaper background. Interlacing strapwork is frequent. Jesse windows occupy one or two lancets at the most.

FOURTEENTH CENTURY

Silver staining is introduced, giving a golden colour to the glass and allowing one portion of the glass only to be coloured. Colours become less rich. Medallions cut into the borders, cross-hatching disappears and some separating lines are painted in instead of being leaded. Saddle bars are used. Grisaille glass has coloured or white border round each tracery. Heraldry appears and canopied figures standing sometimes on tiled paving. Borders depict fleur-de-lys and oak leaf, the foliage naturally drawn. The canopies have cusped arches and crocketted gables. Jesse windows ignore the mullions. Black letter or Gothic lettering appears. Stippling is used in the latter part of the century.

FIFTEENTH CENTURY

Flash glass comes in; that is, one surface of a piece of white glass is coated with colour, and by scratching or abrading this colour the white glass is exposed. Much gold appears in the windows, the nimbus being contained in the same piece as the face. Diamond quarries have separate drawings and lights are divided horizontally, the mullions dividing vertically. Figures stand on chequered paving, with distant landscape in perspective. Canopies have pinnacles, but are often omitted, and drapery flows. Flesh is depicted by white glass. Subjects are shown in groups, occupying several lights. Often the donor is portrayed and heraldic detail is frequent. Angels, holding shields, occupy the tracery.

SIXTEENTH CENTURY

Figures are boldly coloured on white ground and canopies are enlarged. Prominence is given to scenery which is shown in perspective, the leads no longer contributing to the design, often seeming to imprison the figures. Angels and cherubs are common subjects, and in rose windows the figures occupy the centre and the outer lights are treated as tracery. Other features are scrollwork, needlepoint etching and annealing, i.e. a piece of coloured glass fixed by heating to an uncoloured pane.

SEVENTEENTH CENTURY

The art declines. Much prominence is given to the donor who is shown with his family, father and sons kneeling on one side, mother and daughters on the other. Windows become painted pictures.

X. ARCHITECTURAL GLOSSARY

See illustrations on pages 45–47

ABACUS: upper member of the capital of a column, generally in the form of a square slab on which rests the architrave or foot of the arch supported by the column.

ABBEY: monastery under the rule of an abbot.

ABUTMENT: part of a wall sustaining an arch.

ACANTHUS: leaf moulding characteristic of Grecian architecture.

AISLE: lateral division separated from the nave by the arcade.

ALTAR: table of wood or stone used for the celebration of the Lord's Supper.

AMBO: pulpit, situated normally one either side of the sanctuary and used for the reading of Epistle and Gospel at Communion. Also found on occasions in the monastic refectory where one of the community would read aloud during meals.

AMBULATORY: passageway behind the sanctuary giving access to the shrine or to chapels.

APSE: semicircular termination of the arm of a church building, roofed by a semi-dome or contained in the thickness of the wall.

ARCADE: series of arches supported by columns or formed in a wall. A BLIND ARCADE is a series of arches sculptured on the face of a wall.

ARCHITRAVE: beam resting on columns; moulded frame of an opening.

ARCUATED: arched construction in contrast to beamed construction.

ASHLAR: hewn stones.

AUMBRY: cupboard; in particular, a cupboard set in the wall of the sanctuary or placed on the high altar in which a portion of the sacramental bread and wine is retained to be taken to the sick.

BALDACCHINO: canopy over altar, upheld by pillars.

BALLFLOWER: small ornament cut from solid—a berry in an opening, four-petalled flower: a feature of fourteenth-century Gothic.

BALUSTER: vertical member supporting a rail.

BALUSTRADE: row of banisters or coping ornamenting a parapet.

BAPTISTRY: a building or part of a church used for baptisms.

BAR TRACERY: interlacing ribwork of slender shafts continuing the lines of the mullion: a feature of thirteenth-century Gothic.

BARREL VAULT: semicircular vaulting deriving its name from its likeness to the inside of a barrel, the curvation formed by the mortar: a feature of Romanesque architecture.

BEAKHEAD: Romanesque moulding.

BELFRY: tower in which bells are hung or the room in a tower sheltering the bells.

BILLET: moulding of short rolls cut in a hollow moulding: a feature of Romanesque architecture.

BLACK LETTERING: painted lettering used on stained glass during and after the fourteenth century.

BLIND STORY: *see* TRIFORIUM.

BOSS: keystone at intersection of ribs, often elaborately carved.

BROACH SPIRE: one which springs from the edges of the tower without parapet.

BUTTRESS: support built against a wall.

CADAVER: carved or sculptured representation of a decaying corpse.

CAMPANILE: bell-tower.

CANDELABRA: large, branched candlestick.

CAPITAL: upper member of a column.

CHANTRY: chapel endowed for the offering of masses for the donor's soul, sometimes containing the tomb which may serve as the altar.

CHAPTER HOUSE: originally a monastic room where the community met daily to hear the reading of a chapter of the Rule of St. Benedict. Latterly a room where dean and canons, or prior and monks, meet for the discussion of business.

CHEVET: group of chapels encircling an eastern apse and radiating from an ambulatory: a feature of French Gothic design.

CHEVRON: zigzag moulding: a feature of Romanesque architecture.

CHOIR: that part of the cathedral seating the singers, at the crossing or within the chancel.

CINQUEFOIL: arch divided by cusps into five divisions.

CLERESTORY: upper portion of the aisle wall, pierced by windows.

COFFERING: sunken panels in vood, plaster or stucco ceiling.

CORBEL: shelf of stone or wood projecting from a wall.

CORBEL TABLE: series of corbels bearing a continuous shelf or stringcourse.

CORNICE: horizontal projection.

CRENELATION: battlement-like parapet.

CROCKET: curled leaf ornamentation.

CROZIER: crook-shaped staff symbolic of episcopal office.

CRYPT: underground chamber.

CUSP: projecting point at the meeting of two arches.

DIAPER: ornamental design of repeated, patterned squares or diamonds, possibly copied from tapestry work.

DIAPHRAGM ARCH: arch traversing a nave, but not carrying the weight of the vault.

DIOCESE: territory under the jurisdiction of a bishop.

DOGTOOTH: pyramidal ornament cut in the solid: a feature of Romanesque architecture.

DORTER: monastic dormitory.

DOWEL: wooden pin.

DRIPSTONE: projection over an exterior doorway to protect from rain.

EASTER SEPULCHRE: cavity normally in the north wall of the sanctuary where the sacrament was placed between Good Friday and Easter Day.

ENCAUSTIC TILE: one into which the design has been burned.

ENTABLATURE: beam born by columns.

EXTRADOS: upper surface of an arch.

FAÇADE: frontage facing an approach.

FAN VAULT: decorative vaulting formed by ribs of similar curvation set at equal angles: a feature of Perpendicular Gothic.

FERETORY: chest containing relics of a saint or that part of the church where the shrine is situated.

FILLET: narrow band of stone separating two mouldings.

FINIAL: ornamental termination of a gable, canopy or stall.

FLYING BUTTRESS: buttress of two members, the lower arched, the upper straight, the space between the two sometimes filled, springing from a buttress to support a wall or vault.

FOUR-CENTRED ARCH: a pointed arch of which the voussoirs spring from two 'pairs' of centres.

FRATER: monastic dining-room.

FRESCO: pattern painted on to plaster before the plaster is dry.

GALILEE: name given to a chapel situated at the west end of the cathedral.

GARGOYLE: rain spout grotesquely carved.

GRAFFITO: designs scratched on plaster or stone.

GRISAILLE: grey-coloured glass of thirteenth and fourteenth centuries.

GROIN: meeting-point of the two edges of adjoining vaults.

HALL CHURCH: one in which the aisles rise to the full height of the nave.

HAMMERBEAM: horizontal cantilever supporting roof beam.

HOOD MOULDING: projection above internal opening.

IMPOST: upper portion of column from which an arch springs.

INTRADOS: lower surface of an arch, soffit.

JAMB: side post of door or window.

JUBE: rood loft dividing nave from choir.

KEYSTONE: summit stone of an arch.

LABEL: dripstone or hood moulding having vertical side mouldings.

LADY CHAPEL: chapel dedicated to the Blessed Virgin Mary.

LANCET: narrow, pointed window.

LANTERN: tower pierced by windows.

LIERNE: short, decorative ribs not springing from the abacus or central boss.

LOMBARDIC LETTERING: scratched lettering used on stained glass before fourteenth century.

LUCARNE: small, gabled window in a spire.

MISERERE, MISERICORD: corbel or bracket on underside of hinged choir seat, often decoratively carved, offering partial support while standing. (Latin *misericordia*, pity.)

MITRE: bishop's two-pointed head-dress symbolic of the descent of the Holy Spirit in the likeness of cloven tongues.

MOULDING: sculptured or carved ornamentation.

MULLION: vertical bar dividing window lights.

NARTHEX: porch or vestibule.

NAVE: body of the western limb of the church. (Greek *naos* temple.)

NICHE: recess for the accommodation of a statue.

NIMBUS: halo.

OGRE ARCH: arch having concave curve below and convex curve above: a feature of fourteenth-century Gothic.

ORIEL WINDOW: window projecting from an upper story, a feature of sixteenth-century architecture.

OSSUARY: building, or part of a building, containing bones of the dead.

PARCLOSE SCREEN: screen surrounding a tomb or chantry chapel.

PECTORAL CROSS: small pendant cross worn on the chest by a bishop.

PEDIMENT: triangular or curved head of a portico or façade.

PENDENTIVE: concave triangle of in-filling or stone joining the extradoses of two arches standing at right angles.

PEW: bench with back.

PIER: solid masonry support of vault or tower.

PILASTER: column attached to a wall; rudimentary buttress.

PISCINA: stone basin usually attached to the south wall of the sanctuary, used for the washing of the Communion vessels. In early centuries the word was used to indicate a font.

PLATE TRACERY: window headstone pierced by decorative tracery.

PLINTH: lower portion of the base of a column, normally square.

POPPYHEAD: ornamental finial of desk or bench.

PRESBYTERY: that part of the building reserved for the seats of the clergy, often synonymous with the chancel.

PRIORY: monastic house ruled by a prior.

PULPITUM: solid screen of stone separating nave from choir, normally placed between the eastern piers of the crossing, to give privacy to the services attended by the canons or monks. Often used as an organ gallery.

PUTTI: cherub.

QUARRY: diamond-shaped pane of glass.

QUOIN: corner-stone or external angle of a building.

REBUS: carving suggestive of a name.

REFECTORY: monastic dining-room.

REREDOS: screen backing an altar.

RETABLE: shelf decorated with panels backing an altar.

RETROCHOIR: that part of the cathedral east of the sanctuary, frequently sheltering the shrine.

RIB: moulding supporting an arcuated wall or vault.

RIDGE: juncture of two inclined surfaces.

ROOD: crucifix.

ROOD LOFT, ROOD SCREEN: loft or screen bearing a crucifix, normally placed between the western piers of the crossing. *See also* JUBE.

ROUNDEL: disc or medallion of glass.

RUSTICATION: roughened masonry with deeply recessed mortar joints.

SACRISTY: room used for the preparation of the Communion vessels; vestry.

SADDLE BARS: vertical metal bars supporting panels of stained glass: sondlets: stanchions.

SANCTUARY: that part of the cathedral where the altar stands.

SANCTUARY KNOCKER: ornamental knocker allowing accused persons to seek refuge in the church while awaiting trial or extradiction.

SCALLOP; SCOLLOP: shell-like moulding.

SEDILIA: seat; normally three seats placed on the south side of the sanctuary for the officiating ministers.

SEE: diocese.

SHINGLES: rectangles of wood used as roofing tiles.

SLYPE: tunnel-like passageway.

SOFFIT: *see* INTRADOS.

SONDLETS: *see* SADDLE BARS.

SPANDREL: triangular in-filling adjoining the shoulder of an arch.

SPIRE: tapering pyramid or cone crowning a tower.

SQUINCH ARCH: arch placed across an interior angle to form an octagonal support for a dome.

SQUINT: window or opening cut obliquely to afford view of an altar.

STALACTITE: cone structure dependent from vault: a feature of sixteenth-century Gothic.

STALL: fixed seat or bench with backing.

STANCHION: *see* SADDLE BAR.

STEEPLE: spire.

STELLAR VAULTING: lierne vaulting arranged to present a star-like appearance.

STILTED ARCH: elongation of imposts to gain height.

STOUP: basin.

STRINGCOURSE: horizontal projection on exterior wall.

STYLOBITE: continuous base supporting columns.

TABERNACLE-WORK: canopies.

TERRA-COTTA: pottery formed of baked earth.

TESSELLATED PAVING: paving formed of mosaics.

TESSERA: small cube of glass or stone used in mosaic work.

TESTER: canopy, normally pendent over shrine or altar.

TIERCHON: intermediate vaulting rib.

TRABEATED: beam structure in contrast to arcuated.

TRACERY: ornamental stonework in the head of a window.

TRANSEPT: lateral projection of a cruciform cathedral normally between nave and choir, but sometimes found in addition either side of the choir.

TRANSITIONAL STYLE: one style modified by or embracing features of a succeeding style.

TRANSOM: horizontal bar.

TREFOIL: triple-lobed tracery.

TRICHORA: three-apsed termination.

TRIFORIUM: upper stage of nave wall, normally without windows, with arched openings on to a gallery. *See also* CLERESTORY.

TRUMEAU: pillar dividing a doorway.

TYMPANUM: triangular or semi-circular stonework or infilling crowning a door or window.

UNDERCROFT: crypt or room beneath an upper room.

VAULT: arched roof.

VESICA: pointed, oval opening.

VESTRY: room used for the robing of the clergy.

VOLUTE: ornamentation in the form of a partially unrolled scroll: a feature of Grecian architecture.

VOUSSOIRS: wedge-shaped stones forming an arch.

WICKET GATE: small door or gate within a larger one.

'SE

BOSS

BUTTRESS

RCADE

ARCHES

Drop · Lancet · Equilateral

Pointed
Trefoil · Ogee · Four
Centred

Cinquefoil · Multifoil

**CLEAR STORY
or Clerestory**

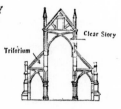

Triforium · Clear Story

CORNICE

FLYING BUTTRESS

CROCKETS

CUSPS

GARGOYLE

FINIAL

FLAMBOYANT TRACERY

MOULDINGS

Early English

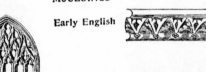

Perpendicular

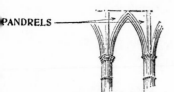

PANDRELS

WINDOWS

Decorated
(Flowing Tracery)

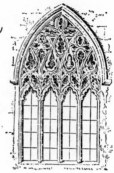

VAULTS

Groined with moulded ribs

Perpendicular

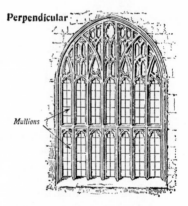

Mullions

XI. THE ENGLISH CATHEDRAL FOUNDATIONS

BIRMINGHAM: Parish Church
BLACKBURN: Parish Church
BRADFORD: Parish Church
BRISTOL: Augustinian Abbey
BURY ST. EDMUNDS: Parish Church
CANTERBURY: Benedictine Monks
CARLISLE: Benedictine Monks
CHELMSFORD: Parish Church
CHESTER: Benedictine Monks.
CHICHESTER: Secular Canons
COVENTRY: New Foundation.
DERBY: Parish Church
DURHAM: Benedictine Monks
ELY: Benedictine Monks
EXETER: Secular Canons
GLOUCESTER: Benedictine Monks
GUILDFORD: New Foundation
HEREFORD: Secular Canons
LEICESTER: Parish Church
LICHFIELD: Secular Canons
LINCOLN: Secular Canons
LIVERPOOL: New Foundation
LONDON: St. Paul's: New Foundation
MANCHESTER: Parish Church
NEWCASTLE: Parish Church
NORWICH: Benedictine Monks
OXFORD: Augustinian Priory
PETERBOROUGH: Benedictine Monks
PORTSMOUTH: Parish Church
RIPON: Secular Canons
ROCHESTER: Benedictine Monks
ST. ALBANS: Benedictine Monks
SALISBURY: Secular Canons
SHEFFIELD: Parish Church
SOUTHWARK: Augustinian Priory
SOUTHWELL: Secular Canons
TRURO: New Foundation
WAKEFIELD: Parish Church
WELLS: Secular Canons
WINCHESTER: Benedictine Monks
WORCESTER: Benedictine Monks
YORK: Secular Canons

XII. THE ROMAN NUMERALS AND THE LITURGICAL COLOURS

THE ROMAN NUMERALS

$$I = 1 \qquad V = 5 \qquad X = 10$$
$$L = 50 \qquad C = 100 \qquad D = 500 \qquad M = 1,000$$

THE LITURGICAL COLOURS

It is normally, but not invariably, the custom in the Western Church to display symbolic colours at the varying seasons of the Church's year—in the altar frontal and the vestments of the ministers.

WHITE is used at Christmas, Easter, Ascension. It is also used on feastdays of the Virgin Mary and on those of saints who have not died by martyrdom. It is the colour of joy and of purity. GOLD is sometimes used for white.

PURPLE or BLUE is the colour of sorrow and is used at such times when Christians are called to repentance in preparation for the Greater Festivals: Advent in preparation for Christmas; Lent in preparation for Easter.

RED is used at Whitsuntide, a reminder of the descent of the Holy Spirit in the form of tongues of fire. It is also used on the days when martyrs are commemorated.

GREEN, the colour of creation, is used when none of the above colours are appropriate.

D

XIII. THE ENGLISH CATHEDRALS

BIRMINGHAM

The cathedral, occupying a pleasant position among trees in the city centre, is the only building of any age left in the vicinity. It was built in 1711 in the Neo-Classical style to the design of Thomas Archer, and was adopted as the cathedral on the formation of the diocese in 1905.

The site, once a part of Barley Close Farm, was the gift of a Mr. Phillips, in recognition of which it was dedicated to St. Philip.

EXTERIOR

A balustrade ornamented with Grecian urns decorates the roof. Windows and entrances are insignificant. The tower has concave sides and pilasters with Doric capitals, the lantern being crowned by a weathervane depicting the arms of the Gough family. Sir Richard Gough persuaded George II to donate £600 towards the cost of building.

INTERIOR

The nave is separated from the aisles by arcades of coffered arches supported by gilded, fluted piers with Doric capitals, with massive plinths, their design somewhat marred by the intervening galleries. The prominent cornice is decorated with gilding.

Archer's original shallow chancel was replaced by the present one in 1884, curved walls and pillars with Doric capitals harmonizing with the nave piers. The tower was opened to provide a baptistry.

The notable Burne-Jones windows were installed during the last quarter of the nineteenth century. The artist was a native of Birmingham and was baptized in the cathedral. The waist-high screen of wrought iron separating the chancel has been attributed to Jean Tijou, who, during the reign of William and Mary, worked under the patronage of the queen, and contributed screenwork to Hampton Court Palace and St. Paul's Cathedral. The organ case dates from 1715. In 1765 the organist was Jeremiah Clarke, the composer of 'Purcell's' Trumpet Voluntary.

BLACKBURN

The site is reputed to have been occupied by a Saxon church, but the first mention of a church is in Doomsday Book. A Norman church was rebuilt in the fourteenth and again in the sixteenth centuries, leaving no remains in either case. The present building, which became the cathedral of the new diocese in 1926, dates from 1818 and has recently been greatly extended, with the addition of attractive colouring and modern sculpture.

EXTERIOR

The pinnacled Gothic tower, nave and aisles belong to the nineteenth-century building and are among the earliest fruits of the Gothic revival. The new extension is marked by a lantern tower surmounted by a slender flèche. The western doors are ornamented with striking, gilded carvings of Christ in Glory and the diocesan arms. The tympanums of the flanking doors show the Annunciation and the Nativity.

INTERIOR

The nineteenth-century nave has slender columns and a ribbed vault, with ornamental bosses and corbels. In the spacious modern sanctuary the free-standing altar, lighted by the new lantern, has a corona bearing sanctuary lamps. The west end is dominated by John Hayward's figure of Christ the Worker.

A chapel with etched glass screen is dedicated to St. Martin of Tours. In the transept is a fibreglass reproduction of the Madonna and Child depicted on a fifteenth-century pyx discovered in the churchyard. The north window has nineteenth-century Flemish glass and the south glass reassembled from the original nave windows; other windows preserve fragments of medieval glass.

BRADFORD

The cathedral, its position cramped by surrounding buildings, was the product of the prosperous wool trade, being the parish church of the city before being adopted as the cathedral.

EXTERIOR

The tower, erected at the close of the fifteenth century, is the most pleasing feature of an undistinguished building.

INTERIOR

The roof of the nave has been ornamented with heraldic shields and angel corbels. The transepts were added at the end of the last century and there are modern extensions at the east end.

BRISTOL

This is remarkable as being the only example of a hall church in the country.

Founded in 1140 as an abbey in charge of Augustinian Canons, it was consecrated twenty-five years later. A charter granted by Henry II about 1153 refers to his visit to the abbey in 1142. At the dissolution of the monasteries the church became, in 1542, the cathedral of a new diocese.

EXTERIOR

Adjacent to the cathedral is the gateway of the abbey, restored in the sixteenth century, but retaining the original masonry of its lower portion. The central tower dates from the fifteenth century, but the western towers are nineteenth-century restorations.

INTERIOR

The nave was rebuilt in the sixteenth century, but the work was interrupted by the dissolution of the monasteries and left unfinished and roofless. Walled off from the chancel, it was allowed to become ruinous until restored last century, its design harmonizing with that of the original choir.

The crossing, with attractive vaulting reflecting that of the choir, and both transepts were erected in the fifteenth century, but the south transept has its fourteenth-century walls and the night stairs remain, originally giving access to the monastic dormitory. On the adjacent wall is displayed a Saxon coffin lid richly carved.

The choir was built between 1298 and 1330. It has a finely ornamented vault. The stalls retain some of their original carving and magnificent misericords. The choir aisles display interesting vaulting, with stone bridges taking the thrust of the walls. There are finely sculptured stellar grave-recesses. The beautiful choir screen was presented in 1542, having belonged to a Carmelite priory.

The church is remarkable for possessing two Lady Chapels, that known as 'the Elder' adjacent to the north choir aisle was erected as a free-standing chapel in 1215 and later joined to the church. The capitals of the pillars are richly carved. The tombstone of its builder, Abbot David, lies near its entrance.

The Eastern Lady Chapel is of the same date as the choir, 1320. Its lierne vaulting is the earliest known. The stellar recesses, their medieval colouring brilliantly restored, and the restored sedilia are of great magnificence. The altar has its original reredos, but with the addition of a sixteenth-century parapet. The candlesticks are early eighteenth century. Note the rebus of Abbot Bruton and the cadaver tomb of the first bishop (d. 1553).

From the south aisle access is gained through a finely vaulted vestibule to the Berkeley Chapel where the Berkeley tomb is enriched by magnificent stellar carving. The fifteenth-century paintings on the south-east window jambs should be noted, and the medieval candelabra.

A modern doorway gives access to the cloisters which retain an original wall and fragments of medieval glass in the window borders. The Romanesque vestibule of the Chapter House displays both round and pointed arches, while the twelfth-century Chapter House is richly decorated with interlacing blind arcading and sculptured ribs; its eastern wall is a nineteenth-century restoration. Other remains of the monastic buildings include the refectory and the slype.

BURY ST. EDMUNDS

In 855 the young Edmund landed at Hunstanton to receive the crown of the kingdom of East Anglia. A Christian monastery had then existed at Bury—or Beodricsworth, as it was called—for the previous two centuries. During his reign the vicious, pagan raids of the Vikings developed into a war of conquest. In 870 Edmund was captured by the enemy and, refusing to deny his faith, was brutally murdered. In 903 his body was conveyed to a new wooden church at Beodricsworth to be known in future as Bury St. Edmunds.

In 1032 a new church was erected and the secular clergy in charge of the shrine replaced by monks. Yet a further church was built in 1095. The monastery was soon to become one of the wealthiest and most famed in the country.

The present cathedral church was founded by the seventh abbot, Anselm, as compensation for his inability to make a pilgrimage to the shrine of St. James in Spain. In 1438 the rebuilding of this church was commenced, but not completed until the reign of Edward VI. Much alteration and rebuilding has taken place during the present century.

EXTERIOR

The church is dominated by the bell-tower erected in the twelfth century as the main entrance to the abbey. Some remains of the third abbey church of 1095 are to be seen in the churchyard, while some of the stone drums from the first Church of St. James, founded in the twelfth century, are visible in the north wall. The scallop shell, wallet and staff, emblems of pilgrims and of St. James, are sculptured on the west front.

INTERIOR

The nave dates from 1438, though not completed until the following century. The hammerbeam roof is a nineteenth-century replacement and has been enriched with colouring in recent times, shields carrying symbols of the patron saint and St. Edmund. The crossing, transepts, choir and chapels belong to the twentieth century; heraldic shields bear the arms of the barons who in 1214 met at the abbey for the signing of Magna Carta.

The modern font has a cover of exceptional beauty. At the west end are displayed the gilded cherub from the old organ case and the seventeenth-century arms of Charles II. Porch and cloisters have also been added in the present century. The great west window has modern stained glass. The jesse window at the west end of the south aisle contains fifteenth-century glass in its lower lights.

CANTERBURY

In 597 Augustine landed in Kent accompanied by a large party of monks and in the same year baptized Ethelbert, the local king. On a site at Canterbury he erected the first cathedral, an oblong building with a crypt and at either end an apse. While the eastern apse held an altar, the chief altar appears to have been situated in front of the western apse where the cathedra was placed. There were towers north and south, beneath one of which was the entrance porch. In 741 a detached baptistry was added.

With the coming of the Normans, the Saxon cathedral was demolished and rebuilt by Lanfranc, the archbishop, who found the church in a ruinous condition its remains having been gutted by fire in 1067. With remarkable speed it was rebuilt in Caen stone within the next seven years. Now it was given a central tower flanked by transepts and a nave marked by a gilded lantern and terminating in twin towers with golden pinnacles. Lanfranc placed it in the charge of Benedictine monks.

In the following century the nave was rebuilt on a greater scale and the Norman choir, destroyed by fire in 1174, was re-erected early in the following century to a lavish design to contain the relics of the murdered Archbishop Thomas à Becket. The present nave, set at a slight angle to the choir, was erected two hundred years later. The ascending levels as it progresses from nave to eastern corona chapel are an outstanding feature of the cathedral.

EXTERIOR

The western front, flanked by its pinnacled towers, belongs to the fifteenth century, though the north-west tower is a nineteenth-century restoration.

The great central tower, one of the loveliest in the country and known as the Bell Harry, was erected in the late fifteenth century, the master-mason being John Wastell, who was afterwards concerned in the building of the cathedral at Bury St. Edmunds. It is 235 ft. in height.

Among the sparse relics of the Norman monastery are the steps which once led to the guest-house, now incorporated in the cathedral school. The first school was founded in 631.

Also there remains the circular twelfth-century water-tower.

The eastern termination of the church is of particular interest, forming a chevet with the corona chapel as its eastern chapel in contrast to the normal square ending of the English cathedral. The chevet reflects the influence of a French master-mason, William of Sens.

INTERIOR

The magnificent nave was built in 1410, the Romanesque pillars of the earlier structure being encased in Gothic mouldings. A bay of the northern arcade contains the seventeenth-century font.

The splendid pulpitum, ornamented with the figures of kings, belongs to the early fifteenth century. North of the pulpitum is the transept known as the Martyrdom, where Becket was struck down.

It was here in 1170 that the four knights, coming from the cloister, encountered the archbishop in the grey twilight. Robert le Breton broke his sword against a pillar as he severed Becket's scalp and Hugh de Morville scattered the archbishop's brains upon the paving. Gathered ghoulishly by the monks into a vessel, both scalp and brains were to be preserved as holy relics in the eastern chapel, while the hair shirt 'crawling with vermin' would be kissed by countless pilgrims.

To the north, the Lady Chapel was erected in 1450. Beside it is the entrance to the crypt where Becket's shrine was first placed and where Henry knelt and was flogged as a self-imposed penance.

This is the largest Norman crypt in the world, belonging to the twelfth-century building. The capitals of the pillars should be noted. In 1952 mural paintings dating from the twelfth century were discovered in the crypt chapel of St. Gabriel and have been beautifully restored.

The choir above was rebuilt in 1180 by William of Sens; he was crippled in a fall from the scaffolding before it was completed and that part beyond the high altar is the work of his successor, William the Englishman, and was finished early in the thirteenth century. Although contemporary with the Angel Choir of Lincoln and the west front of Wells, it reflects neither the delicacy of the former nor the grandeur of the latter.

Archbishop Chichele's magnificent tomb, with cadaver, adjacent to the transept, has its colouring brilliantly restored.

The chapels of the north transept are dedicated to St. Martin and St. Stephen.

Eastwards, steps lead into the ambulatory which gives access to Trinity Chapel, where Becket's shrine was finally placed, its position marked by mosaic paving. 'A coffin of wood which covered a coffin of gold was drawn up by ropes, and then an invaluable treasure was discovered: gold was the meanest thing to be seen there; all shone and glittered with the rarest and most precious jewels of an extraordinary size; some were larger than the egg of a goose . . .'

In a watching chamber above St. Anselm's Chapel monks, with guard dogs, did sentry duty, and when Henry VIII destroyed the shrine it required twenty-six carts to move the jewels and precious metals.

Further east, Henry IV's tomb has a painted tester, and in the corona chapel stands the 'enthronement chair' of the archbishops; though called Augustine's chair, it dates from the early thirteenth century.

Beyond the worn pilgrim stairs, westward, stands the tomb of the Black Prince, with handsome effigy and helmet, surcoat and gauntlets, displayed nearby.

The Warrior Chapel shelters the grave of Stephen Langton and has the earliest lierne vault in England. There is delicate fan-vaulting above the crossing.

The cloisters, placed unusually on the north, are complete, erected in 1073, but reconstructed at the end of the following century. The vaulting, rich with heraldic arms, dates from 1400.

The northern cloister gives access to the fourteenth-century Chapter House, with magnificent oaken roof.

Canterbury Cathedral has been described as the greatest treasury of stained glass in England. A considerable amount of thirteenth-century glass is preserved. The lowest lights in the great west window are thirteenth century, the upper of similar date to the window itself: early fifteenth century. Adjacent to the place once occupied by the shrine, on the north side, a medallion of 1200 depicts a likeness of the arch-bishop, while another light shows the shrine itself. The choir clerestory, the east window in the corona chapel and the south transept contain ancient glass. There are also fine examples of modern stained glass.

The choir stalls are late seventeenth century and have rich tabernacle work. The use of purbeck shafts in the choir is notable as being the earliest use of that Dorset stone in cathedral building.

CARLISLE

In the seventh century Cuthbert, as Bishop of Lindisfarne in Northumberland, cared for a diocese which stretched the width of England. It is possible, therefore, that he visited the area around Carlisle, but it was not until the twelfth century that the first church was built there. In 1123 a priory of Augustinian Canons was founded which, ten years later, was made the seat of a bishopric.

During the Middle Ages, the city was constantly engulfed in border warfare; the crippled cathedral church bears witness to a history fraught with disasters. Twice—in the thirteenth and fourteenth centuries—the building has been partially destroyed by fires. In the seventeenth-century war against Scotland the monastic buildings were wantonly destroyed, and a hundred years later, during the Jacobite rising, the church became a prison.

EXTERIOR

The undistinguished central tower is Norman in origin, but in 1401 received a Perpendicular casing and at the same time was heightened. The remnant of the Norman nave is further marred by ugly buttresses.

The east wall, with its immense window, is of interesting design aimed to disguise the fact that the window is not centrally placed in relation to the gable. There is a statue of the Virgin and Child, to whom the cathedral is dedicated, above the window, and buttress niches hold statues of four apostles.

The remains of the monastic buildings are on the south side of the church. The Fratery was built in 1350, but rebuilt the following century. It has a west window of notable design and a wall pulpit. A Tower of Refuge, the upper floor of which was the prior's lodging, has massive walls and was probably intended as a protective shelter when border raids were frequent.

INTERIOR

A nineteenth-century doorway gives access to the remains of the Norman church where immense columns support the tower. Only 40 ft. of the original 140-ft. nave remain, now occupied by a military chapel with handsome wrought-iron screen. Subsidence, occurring during the actual building of the tower, caused the northern piers to sink and has left a misshapen triforium above, but the clerestory was added after the settlement had taken place.

While the south transept is of the same date as the nave, that on the north is fifteenth century. St. Catherine's Chapel in the former transept is of the same date as the choir and has a delicate fifteenth-century screen.

The first rebuilding of the choir took place in the thirteenth century, and of this the outer walls of the choir aisles remain. But fire caused a second rebuilding in the following century and the choir itself and the eastern termination belong to this period. It is separated from the crossing by a fifteenth-century pulpitum and from the north aisle by a sixteenth-century screen.

The immense fourteenth-century east window has original glass in the tracery, and the fifteenth-century canopied choir stalls have splendid misericords.

The backs of the stalls are decorated with fifteenth-century paintings depicting the lives of St. Antony, St. Augustine and St. Cuthbert, while the capitals of the pillars have delightful sculptures representing the months of the year, though unfortunately half of these are hidden by the stalls.

Also to be noted are the sixteenth-century pulpit, the thirteenth-century effigy of the bishop in the north choir aisle, the seventeenth-century brass in the south choir aisle and the Saxon stone in the south transept.

At the termination of the north choir aisle the modern altar dedicated to St. Michael has colourful riddel post figures of St. Cuthbert and Henry I.

CHELMSFORD

The church became a cathedral on the creation of the diocese in 1914.

EXTERIOR

Like many Essex churches, the building is of flint. It was rebuilt by the townspeople—described as 'liberal willers'—in the fifteenth century, of which building the present tower, now crowned by an eighteenth-century spire, is almost the sole survivor.

At the east end Huxley Jones' St. Peter is dressed in the costume of an Essex fisherman.

INTERIOR

The fifteenth-century porch is patterned in flints and has a carved medieval ceiling and modern stained glass. A room above houses a library.

Two of the western pillars have been hollowed out apparently to provide cupboards. The nave itself was rebuilt, after collapse, last century. The roof has gilded corbel figures.

On the north is the brilliantly coloured Tudor tomb of the Mildmay family, the father with eight sons facing the mother with her nine daughters.

The windows contain modern stained glass of good design.

CHESTER

The first church at Chester was built in 907 to shelter the relics of a royal nun, St. Werburgh. It was in the charge of a college of priests who, in addition to maintaining the worship of the church, formed a group ministry serving the surrounding villages. But in Norman times, with the support of Archbishop Anselm, these secular canons were replaced by Benedictine monks who immediately demolished the Saxon church and replaced it by a building of which remnants are still to be seen.

The monks continued to honour the parochial responsibilities of the original foundation and allowed the south aisle of the nave to be used as a parish church, an arrangement which persisted into the fourteenth century.

The monastery was dissolved in 1540 and the church became the cathedral of a new diocese. From the seventeenth century to the last century the south transept was the parish church.

The church was almost entirely rebuilt between the thirteenth and the sixteenth centuries, since when much restoration has been carried out which has not always been to the improvement of the building.

The remains of the monastic buildings are extensive.

EXTERIOR

The west front dates from the early sixteenth century, as does also the upper portion of the central tower.

The intention was to provide the church with western towers, but this was never realized, only the ground story being erected. The south-west porch was built in 1508.

The abbey gateway stands a short distance to the north of the church.

INTERIOR

The north arcade of the nave and the generous clerestory windows are of the fifteenth and sixteenth centuries, while the south arcade is fourteenth century.

Remains of the twelfth-century church are to be seen in the north-west corner, now the baptistry with a Venetian font, but the most striking remains, dating from the eleventh century, are the rugged arch and Romanesque triforium preserved in the north transept. The fine wooden roof is early sixteenth century.

Nave and choir are separated by a nineteenth-century screen, with modern rood figures, replacing the original stone pulpitum.

The choir is fourteenth century. The stalls are among the glories of the cathedral, with fine tabernacle work and delightful misericords, dating from 1390. The termination of the abbot's stall and the carved figure of a pilgrim are noteworthy.

Richly worked wrought-iron gates of sixteenth-century Spanish workmanship admit to the choir aisles. At the eastern termination is the thirteenth-century Lady Chapel with the base of the shrine of St. Werburgh made about 1310.

The south transept as far as the height of the triforium is fourteenth century, its four altars now restored. The proximity of the monastic buildings prevented the building of a similar transept on the north. There are some modern and amusing corbels decorating the south transept.

The truncated south-west tower is above the Consistory Court, which is furnished attractively with oaken screens, seats and table of 1636.

Two thirteenth-century doorways give access from the north aisle of the nave to the cloister in which is the twelfth-century chapel of the abbot, its vault enriched by decoration of the seventeenth century. The west walk leads to the monastic undercroft or cellar, now fittingly adapted as the cathedral workshop.

The cloisters were first built in the twelfth century, but rebuilt four hundred years later, shortly before the dissolution, and have since been restored. The north walk has its sixteenth-century vault and sculptured bosses. Adjacent is the splendid refectory, with thirteenth-century doorway and arcaded stairway leading to a wall pulpit. The stone dais marks the position of the abbot's table. The east window has modern stonework and attractive stained glass. East of the doorway is the monk's lavatorium.

In the east walk is an attractive thirteenth-century parlour, with slender pillars and ribbed vaulting, and a thirteenth-century vestibule leading into the Chapter House of the same date.

The south walk of the cloisters contains the carrels or cubicles where the monks studied.

CHICHESTER

In 634 Wilfred was born into a noble household in Northumberland. He became a monk and subsequently Bishop of York, but fell into disfavour with the chieftain of Northumberland, was imprisoned and, on his release, banished. He came to Selsey where, as a pioneer missionary to the people, he built a monastery of which the church afterwards became the cathedral of the bishopric of Selsey.

With the coming of the Normans, following William's policy of attaching the bishoprics to the chief centres of population, the cathedral was rebuilt at Chichester in 1091, but destroyed by fire after only twenty-three years. Rebuilt in 1184, much of the church was once again devastated by fire only three years later. It was again reconstructed in 1199. In the following century Richard de Wyche became bishop, endeared himself to his diocese by the humility of his manner of life, and within twenty-three years of his death was a canonized saint, his shrine attracting pilgrims to the cathedral.

EXTERIOR

The free-standing bell-tower is a unique feature of the cathedral. Built in the fifteenth century, it shelters a peal of eight bells, the two oldest having been founded in the sixteenth century.

The west front is thirteenth century, but the lower portions of the two flanking towers were erected a century earlier. The central tower is also thirteenth century, but the original spire collapsed in the last century and the present one is a restoration.

INTERIOR

The nave, with Norman arches springing from massive piers, is of the thirteenth century, the appearance of double aisles lent by the flanking chapels.

The distinctive pulpitum, erected in 1475, was removed when it was apparent that the spire was about to fall last century, and has been restored in recent years.

The north aisle has thirteenth- and fourteenth-century tombs, and there are remnants of medieval mural paintings in the north transept. The window is early fifteenth century.

The choir is fourteenth century. The stalls have fascinating misericords of 1330 which, in contrast to the misericords of practically every other cathedral, are here exposed to view. But the dominating feature of the choir is the magnificent modern tapestry, in brilliant colours, an outstanding work of John Piper, hung behind the altar from a sixteenth-century screen. The chandeliers are of eighteenth-century workmanship.

E

Beyond the choir is the fine twelfth-century retrochoir where once stood the revered shrine of St. Richard. A portion of the vault has sixteenth-century decoration.

The western bays of the Lady Chapel date from 1187. Nearby is the tomb of Bishop Luffa, who died in 1123 and was responsible for the erection of the first Norman church. The eastern bays were built in 1300.

In the south choir aisle are the two most precious possessions of the cathedral: magnificent sculptured tablets probably belonging to the original pulpitum of the Norman church, depicting Christ at the raising of Lazarus.

The south transept has a window of 1325 filled with nineteenth-century glass and a large painting showing Bishop Wilfred at Selsey.

The cathedral is rich in modern works of art: the small, but vibrant Graham Sutherland painting of Mary Magdalene and the risen Christ in the Mary Magdalene chapel, where altar rails and candlesticks are also of modern design, and the effective concrete and aluminium pulpit.

On the south side of the church are the remains of the early fifteenth-century cloisters, with oaken roof and the figure of St. Richard above the western doorway. The refectory of the vicars-choral is to the east, while next to the west end of the church is the fourteenth-century gateway to the bishop's palace.

COVENTRY

The earliest mention of the Church in Coventry is of the destruction of a monastery by Canute. The monastery was refounded in the eleventh century by Earl Leofric and his wife Godiva and placed in the charge of Benedictine monks.

Three hundred years later two brothers and two sisters built a second church, dedicated to St. Michael, of which a rhyme records:

William and Adam built the tower,
Ann and Mary built the spire;
William and Adam built the church,
Ann and Mary built the quire.

The church was enriched with the chapels of the trade guilds, but at the time of the dissolution it was Leofric's and Godiva's church which sheltered the bishop's cathedra, sharing the privilege with Lichfield. Subsequently their church became ruinous and when the bishopric was revived in 1918 St. Michael's was chosen to be the cathedral.

On a November night in 1940 it was largely destroyed by enemy bombers. In 1956 Queen Elizabeth II laid the foundation stone of Sir Basil Spence's new cathedral.

EXTERIOR

The shell of the medieval St. Michael's has been preserved, the position of the high altar marked by the Cross of Nails, formed of nails from the gutted beams. The tower is fourteenth century and has been preserved undamaged.

The south entrance to the new building is marked by Epstein's notable figure of the patron saint, one of the outstanding contributions by contemporary artists whose work has embellished the new church. The great glass doors of the western entrance are etched with the figures of angels.

INTERIOR

The church is built on seven hundred concrete piles, of red sandstone from Staffordshire, with slender columns, the division between nave and sanctuary barely marked.

The choir stalls and cathedra are 'roofed' by a pattern of thorns, and the high altar, flanked by massive stone candlesticks, bears a twisted cross. The body of the church is dominated by the vast Graham Sutherland tapestry of Christ in Glory, the size of which may be gauged by the human figure at its base which is life-size. A thousand shades of wool are woven into the design.

The north aisle has beautifully lettered tablets bearing Gospel texts. The tall, narrow windows are filled with exuberant stained glass only seen as one moves westward from the altar. The south aisle has John Piper's immense and splendid baptistry window, formed of six hundred pieces of coloured glass, illuminating the font formed of a rock from Bethlehem.

The circular Chapel of Unity, designed in the form of a Crusader's tent, has a mosaic floor of great beauty. The Chapel of Industry, successor of the Guild Chapels of the medieval church, contains windows of plain glass, the view through which unites it with the nearby factories and buildings of the city. The Chapel of Gethsemane has a mosaic depicting an angel.

The church, small in size by cathedral standards, is a tribute to the skills of twentieth-century man. It was built in seven years in contrast to the 125 years occupied in the erection of the old St. Michael's.

DERBY

The bishopric was formed in 1927. The parish church adopted as the cathedral is not particularly notable. Designed by James Gibbs, it was built in 1723 and has recently been extended eastwards to form a new sanctuary.

EXTERIOR

The tower is early sixteenth century and is the sole remnant of the original church which, it is said, was otherwise totally demolished overnight by a rector who was in dispute with the city corporation.

INTERIOR

The organ occupies a gallery at the west end and the sanctuary is bounded by a pleasant ironwork screen made locally by Robert Bakewell in the eighteenth century, embellished by the heraldic arms of the House of Hanover. Beyond it, the free-standing altar is sheltered by Sebastian Cowper's new white-pillared baldacchino, an unadorned table of 1623 below the screen doing service as a nave altar. The stained glass in the windows north and south was designed in the present century by Ceri Richards. The choir stalls are set against the eastern wall and a sixteenth-century wooden effigy of a former rector lies below the screen.

A colourful tomb commemorates Bess of Hardwick, who died in 1607 having outlived four husbands and given birth to the founder of the Devonshire family.

DURHAM

The cathedral at Durham, the most wholly Romanesque in the country, is the shrine of St. Cuthbert.

Cuthbert was born in south Scotland in the eighth century, of well-to-do parents, and converted by a vision of St. Aidan. Consecrated unwillingly as bishop, he served a vast diocese stretching the width of northern England before he retired to the Farne Islands as a hermit. He was buried on the Island of Lindisfarne, but in the following centuries, when the raids of pagan Vikings threatened the undefended monastery, the monks disinterred his coffin, placed in it the head of King Oswald and the illuminated Lindisfarne Gospels, and bore it on a prolonged journey through the north, seeking a safe resting-place.

They reached Durham in 995 and were directed by a woman who was searching for her strayed dun cow to the great cliff above the Wear—her sculptured figure is on the exterior north-east corner. Here they built 'a little church of wands and branches' to shelter the coffin, later replaced by a church of stone.

The Normans despised the humble Saxon church and replaced it by a grander one of which the greater part, including some of the monastic buildings, has survived despite the destructive 'restorations' of the notorious Wyatt in the eighteenth century. The shrine became one of the most revered in England. It is recorded that seven thousand masses were said annually by the Benedictine monks who had charge of the church.

The building is remarkable as being basically Romanesque, yet displaying the distinctive features of Gothic architecture: the ribbed vault, the flying buttress and the pointed arch.

The first Norman bishop was murdered by a mob before he could commence building, so that the true founder of the church is the second bishop, William de St. Carileph, who had been inspired by the architecture which he had seen in exile in Normandy. The relics of the eighth-century monk-historian, Bede, were stolen from the ancient Benedictine monastery of Jarrow and presented to Durham. The cost of building was largely financed by the self-sacrifice of the community and the first bishops.

EXTERIOR

The twin western towers are twelfth century, but their battlements were added in the late eighteenth century. The massive buttresses are fifteenth century.

The great central tower was build in 1262, but its wooden spire was struck by lightning and the masonry of the tower badly damaged. One of the monks, armed with a silver crucifix and a piece of St. Cuthbert's shroud, was sent out on a begging tour to raise money for its repair, but it was not until 1470 that it was rebuilt. In the last century Scott removed Wyatt's 'restoration' cement, replaced the statues and added new ones.

The medieval sanctuary knocker on the north-west door is among the unique possessions of the church, though the chambers above were destroyed by Wyatt where 'serten men dyd lie alwaies in two chambers over the said north door, that when any offender dyd come and knocke, straight waie they were letten in, at any houre of the nyght'. Sanctuary—mostly

to homicides—was given for thirty-seven days on condition
the person carried no weapon and wore a special badge; an
oath to abjure the realm was then taken and, holding a white
cross, he was permitted to travel to the nearest port. Twenty
such sanctuary churches existed; at Durham 332 people
sought sanctuary between 1464 and 1524, and the privilege
was abolished in 1624.

INTERIOR

The nave, with its huge, incised, rubble-filled pillars, was
erected in the first half of the twelfth century, its stone vault
an outstanding feature. At the west end a line of black marble
in the paving marks the eastward limit to which women were
allowed access. The inadequate font and its imposing cover
are of the seventeenth century.

Choir and nave are separated by an incongruous screen,
the work of Scott in the last century, replacing a wooden
screen of the seventeenth century which, in turn, replaced the
original stone pulpitum.

Choir and crossing were build in the eleventh century; the
stone vaulting of the aisles is the earliest known.

High on the wall of the choir remain the only two original
statues which escaped the iconoclastic zeal of the Earl of
Somerset. Backing the altar is the lovely fourteenth-century
Neville screen, a fine picture-frame shorn of the picture
which was its *raison d'être*, for it once contained one hundred
and seven alabaster images of saints, all magnificently
coloured. The empty tabernacles of these lost statues indicate
that they were carefully removed, rather than broken, and it
is possible that they are hidden today in some part of the
church or monastic buildings.

The richly carved stalls are seventeenth century, with
misericords, while the brilliantly coloured cathedra, dating
from the fourteenth century, the highest episcopal throne in
Christendom, shelters the later, ornate tomb of Bishop
Hatfield.

Beyond the screen the modern tester marks the position of the grave of Cuthbert, once glorified by a shrine 'exalted with the most curious workmanship, of fine and costly green marble, all limned and gilt with gold', but now a plain stone engraved with the simple title CUTHBERTUS, the nearby paving worn by the genuflecting knees of countless pilgrims.

The body of the saint was reputed to be uncorrupted and a monk had the task of cutting the nails and hair. The grave has been opened on several occasions including once in the last century. The body was then found to lie in the innermost of three coffins which contained also an additional skull—no doubt that of Oswald. A shoulder bone bore the evidence of a boil from which the saint is reputed to have suffered. The remnants of a cloth were gummed to the skull face and the eye-sockets filled with a putty-like substance. Thus it would appear that a pious fraud was perpetrated in medieval times, the body being embalmed, robed in vestments, and the features filled in with putty and covered in cloth.

In the coffin were found a tiny portable altar of silver, the remains of an embroidered stole, the bishop's pectoral cross, a comb and a pair of scissors. These precious relics are now kept in the monastic dormitory.

Efforts had been made to erect a Lady Chapel at the east end, according to custom, but the builders' inability to provide sound foundations had been accepted as proof of Cuthbert's dislike of women! The need for more altars for the celebration of private masses resulted in the addition in the thirteenth century of the Chapel of the Nine Altars, with splendid vaulting, replacing the original apse. Later in the same century a Lady Chapel was erected at the west end, to be known as the Galilee, in which in 1370 was placed the now empty tomb of Bede. The chapel has marble pillars of great delicacy to which stone columns were added early in the fifteenth century. It bears on one of its walls a magnificent twelfth-century painting of Cuthbert. Mercifully the destructive hand of Wyatt was prevented from demolishing the chapel to make a driveway to the western doors.

In the south transept a clock in a fifteenth-century case is carved with a thistle, which is said to have caused its preservation when the church was used as a prison in 1650 for 4,000 starving Scots captured at the battle of Dunbar.

From this transept a handsomely sculptured twelfth-century doorway gave access to the cloisters. The dormitory is the most splendid of the surviving monastic buildings, dating from 1404 and retaining its original roofing. The prior's kitchen still serves the deanery.

The cathedral preserves no ancient glass, but contains at the west end some modern glass which is of interest.

ELY

In 673 Etheldreda, wife of the local king, left her husband, took vows as a nun and founded a monastery for both men and women on the Isle of Ely. After Danish raiders reduced the buildings to ruin it was rebuilt in 970, but again demolished by the Normans and replaced by the present church in 1081. In 1109 the abbot was made first bishop of the see.

EXTERIOR

The west porch is early thirteenth century. The central tower collapsed in 1322 and was rebuilt.

The western tower is also fourteenth century, though the top story was not added until a hundred years later. It appears that originally there was a similar tower on the north-west; an image of St. Etheldreda in the church shows her holding a model of the building which has twin western towers. Strangely, however, there is no record of its removal, which is assumed to have taken place some time in the fourteenth century.

The great gateway of the abbey, built in 1394, is now

incorporated into the school, whose foundation dates back to Saxon times when Edward the Confessor was among its pupils. Apart from this, remains of the monastic buildings are virtually non-existent, cloisters and Chapter House having been destroyed by the Cromwellians. On the south exterior wall of the nave two ornate doorways remain, once giving access to the cloisters.

INTERIOR

The thirteenth-century western doorway is delicately sculptured, with slender central column.

The great nave is late twelfth century and the richly ornamented roof has attractive paintings of the nineteenth century.

The sole surviving relic of Etheldreda's building is the broken column preserved in the south aisle, once part of a memorial to her steward.

The transepts have painted roofs of the fifteenth century, with charmingly carved angels terminating the beams.

The stone pulpitum which originally stood west of the crossing was destroyed at the end of the eighteenth century.

Alan of Walsingham, who was prior in the fourteenth century and whose simple gravestone rests in the nave, was the inspiring genius of the octagon above the crossing. This is the unique and most splendid feature of the cathedral, replacing the central tower after its collapse. Formed of oak trunks 63 ft. in length, weighing 400 tons, for which wide search had to be made and the bridges into Ely strengthened for their transportation, the lantern is an incredible achievement of medieval engineering skill. Sculptured heads of those involved in the work—bishop, prior, master-mason and Alan of Walsingham himself—are at the base of the arches, while the corbels picture the story of the foundress saint.

The choir stands out of alignment with the nave. The western bays, destroyed by the collapse of the central tower and restored at the same date as the construction of the octagon, are distinguished by lierne vaulting and, beyond it, picturesque bosses in the vault of the presbytery mark the position of the saint's shrine. The sale of cheap relics to pilgrims visiting this shrine gave our language the word 'tawdry', derived from St. Awdry, by which name the saint was popularly known.

The choir stalls, once situated below the octagon, are fourteenth century, with original misericords and carved panels added in the nineteenth century.

The presbytery replaced the original apsidal termination of the church and has, either side, fifteenth- and sixteenth-century chantries elaborately decorated. There is a sixteenth-century brass in the south choir aisle.

Until the collapse of the tower the Lady Chapel had been situated in the south aisle. It was now rebuilt on ground adjacent to the north transept and completed in 1349. Flooded with light by immense windows, with stellar vaulting and elaborately arcaded stalls circling its walls, the life of the Blessed Virgin is told in sculptured scenes. With its immense span of roof, the widest of any medieval building, it ranks among the richest achievements of its day, its sculptures once brilliantly coloured and its windows filled with stained glass. After the Reformation and until the present century it was used as a parish church.

All the ancient glass has gone from the cathedral and that which now fills its windows is unremarkable.

Outside the cathedral stands Prior Cauden's Chapel, built in the early part of the fourteenth century; skilfully decorated in its sculpture, it is now the chapel of the school.

EXETER

It is probable that the site of the cathedral was occupied by a monastery in 670. The church was rebuilt in 932 and again in 1019 after destruction by Danish raiders. Meantime, the cathedral at Crediton had also been ravaged by pirates and in the reign of Edward the Confessor the bishopric was moved to Exeter and given into the charge of secular canons.

In the reign of William the Conqueror it was decided to rebuild the church on a larger scale and the completed building was consecrated in 1133. This church in turn was almost entirely rebuilt in the following two centuries.

Built of local stone by Somerset masons, its squat and much-buttressed exterior is unrelieved by any central tower. This is balanced however by the beauty of the interior which contains some of the most magnificent medieval wood carving in the world.

The south choir aisle suffered severe damage in the last war, but has been skilfully restored.

EXTERIOR

The north and south towers were erected in 1133 and, apart from Norman buttresses to the north wall of the nave, are the only relics of the Romanesque structure.

The west front, with its array of numerous statues, all once brilliantly coloured and backed by gilded niches, thirteenth century in date, is much defaced and reflects little of its one-time majesty.

INTERIOR

Entrance to the cathedral is by the north-west porch, the vault of which has fan-vaulting of early fifteenth-century workmanship.

The nave is fourteenth century. One of the ornate bosses in the vaulting depicts the murder of Becket, while a corbel at the east end shows an acrobat making a handstand in honour of the Virgin.

The late seventeenth-century font has an inlaid cover of the same date.

The fourteenth-century minstrels' gallery on the north side, sculptured with an orchestra of angels, is an outstanding feature.

The north transept has a fifteenth-century chantry chapel and a clock of the same date.

Nave and choir are separated by a handsome pulpitum of the fourteenth century, with altars restored in modern times. The arcading of the gallery has seventeenth-century paintings; the chandelier dates from the following century.

The fourteenth-century choir is terminated by twin arches below a splendid window containing some early fourteenth-century glass. The balustrade above the medieval screen is modern.

The dominating feature of the choir is the carved cathedra, 57 ft. in height and built without a single nail. It dates from 1310.

South of the high altar is a fourteenth-century sedilia, with statues of modern design, while on the north side is the tomb of a bishop of the same period. The choir stalls have thirteenth-century misericords and the lectern dates from 1500.

The Lady Chapel is visible beyond the high altar arches. Erected at the close of the thirteenth century, it contains the richly sculptured tomb of the bishop responsible for the building of the present church, also the sculptured effigy of an eleventh-century bishop and a fine sedilia with piscena.

The chapel in the south choir aisle was demolished by a bomb in the last war and has been skilfully restored. At the east termination of the aisle there is a chantry; the 'rebus' owls are to be noted. The chapel has a sculptured corbel of the shepherds.

There are no remaining cloisters. The Chapter House is approached from the south transept and includes the lower walls of the thirteenth-century building, the upper part rebuilt two centuries later, the roof finely painted.

The great church is notable for being in its interior of a single style of architecture, almost wholly dating from the fourteenth century. It is recorded that a scribe was engaged to write out eight hundred indulgences in 1349 to raise money for the work.

GLOUCESTER

The cathedral occupies the site of a seventh-century abbey supposedly built by the Saxon King of Mercia as a penance for the murder of his sons when, contrary to his wishes, they accepted Christianity. The church was rebuilt during the reign of Canute and the secular canons replaced by Benedictine monks. A third rebuilding in 1089 was interrupted by a fire and not completed until 1160. Two hundred years later the monks provided a burial place for the unworthy Edward II, three other abbeys having refused for fear of royal displeasure. The murdered king was popularly accepted as a saint and the multitudes of pilgrims who flocked to his shrine brought immense wealth to the Gloucester monastery, the fruit of which was the birth of Perpendicular architecture with which the Norman church was now adorned. In 1540 the monastery was dissolved and the church re-dedicated as the cathedral.

EXTERIOR

The west front dates from 1420 when the original western towers were demolished.

The south aisle of the nave was reinforced with buttresses in the fourteenth century when the Norman fabric within was refaced in the Perpendicular style.

The central tower was rebuilt in 1450.

At the eastern termination a tunnel was built when the Lady Chapel was extended in the same century.

The fifteenth-century south porch has doors of the twelfth century.

INTERIOR

The nave was completed in 1160, its Romanesque arches supported by immense columns. The vaulting dates from the following century, but the western bays were rebuilt in 1420 and the clerestory windows added.

The ribs of the north and south arches of the crossing were added in 1350. The original stone pulpitum has disappeared.

The south transept is reputedly the birthplace of Perpendicular architecture.

The Norman pillars of the choir were refaced in 1330, the choir raised 25 ft. and completed with fan-vaulting of marvellous delicacy. Of the immense windows that at the east end is of unequalled majesty, preserving its ancient glass commemorating those who fought at Creçy. It is wider than the choir, and the walls are bayed out to receive it. The choir marks the highest achievement of architecture, combining that appearance of weightlessness with the superb unity of style for which architects have aimed from the beginning.

In the centre of the choir reposes the wooden effigy of Duke Robert, eldest of the Conqueror's quarrelsome sons, who was imprisoned by his brother for a quarter of a century in Cardiff Castle. Of the fifty-eight misericords of the stalls forty-four are fourteenth century.

The Lady Chapel was added in the fifteenth century, the eastern window containing remnants of its original glass. The modern glass in the north and south windows is noteworthy. Nearby rests the effigy of murdered Edward beneath its ornate canopy, and a sixteenth-century statute of Saxon Osric, King of Mercia.

In the south transept a sculptured bracket of the fourteenth century commemorates an apprentice who was killed in a fall from the scaffolding. The windows contain some ancient glass.

The crypt, with squat, ponderous columns and low Romanesque arches, survives from the eleventh-century church and sheltered five chapels.

The cloisters are situated north of the nave, which is unusual, and are of outstanding magnificence, with fan-vaulting of unequalled splendour. The north walk has a finely preserved lavatorium and a recess for towels. In the west walk are the carrels or study-cubicles used by the monks, and a stone bench in the east walk has markings which may have been made for a game played by the novices.

The Chapter House was built in the eleventh century and restored in the twelfth; the eastern end dates from the fifteenth century and has Perpendicular vaulting. Here William the Conqueror ordered the writing of Doomsday Book.

Nearby are the remains of a second cloister and of the monastic infirmary.

GUILDFORD

The bishopric was created in 1927 and the foundation stone of Sir Edward Maufe's cathedral was laid nine years later, but its building was interrupted by the war and it was not until 1961 that it was ready for dedication.

It occupies a magnificent site above the city on Stag Hill. The building is entirely of bricks made from local clay.

EXTERIOR

The central tower has a weathervane in the form of a gilded angel with outstretched arm.

The glass doors giving entrance to the western narthex are engraved with angels, and the hand of the Creator is sculptured in the window tracery above.

The south transept has bronze doors sculptured with scenes, and further east the door of St. Ursula's Porch, also of bronze, has handles formed of croziers and angels holding the Diocesan arms.

On the east end is a fine sculpture by Eric Gill symbolizing the Blessed Trinity. Sculptured figures surmount the buttresses.

INTERIOR

The nave is remarkable for its great width, flanked by pointed arches of immense height, with small, recessed clerestory windows above. The narrow aisles rise to the same height as the arcade and act as buttresses.

Five shallow steps form the only division between nave and choir, where a somewhat lowly cathedra, with gilded carving, stands beyond the stalls.

In the nave the north-west pier bears an image of the Madonna and Holy Child and the stairway to the gallery has a charming statue of St. Francis.

A regimental chapel occupies the north transept.

The Lady Chapel, with handsome wrought screen and a finely conceived carved Madonna, forms the eastern termination.

At the western end of the south ambulatory a chapel of impractical design, with miniature altar, is dedicated to children, while the western extremity of the nave aisle has been designed as a rather remote baptistry.

In the sanctuary is a magnificent carpet with woven stag symbolic of Stag Hill on which the cathedral stands.

There is modern stained glass of interesting design.

HEREFORD

The Bishopric of Hereford is reputed to have been in existence in 544, and the bishop to have been among those members of the British Church who held conference with Augustine on the banks of the Severn a few years after his arrival in Kent, but who were repelled by the Italian's pompous manner. Greater certainty, however, attaches to the name of Bishop Putta, who occupied the see in the seventh century.

It is recorded that 'an admirable stone church' was built here in 825 which possibly replaced a former building of wood. In it were preserved the relics of King Ethelbert of

East Anglia, who had been treacherously murdered by the King of Mercia and was held to be a saint by the local people. A new building was erected in 1055, but gutted shortly afterwards by Welsh raiders. The church was restored by the Normans in 1080 and enlarged in the following century.

In 1282 the secular canons who cared for the church obtained the canonization of their bishop, Thomas Cantelope, who had died at Rome and whose chaplain had thoughtfully boiled the corpse and brought the bones back to England. Pilgrimages to the shrine brought new wealth to the cathedral. Thomas Cantelope, who had been Treasurer of England, was the last Englishman to be canonized by the pope before the Reformation.

After a long period of neglect, the church was restored— not very happily—by Wyatt in the eighteenth century.

EXTERIOR

The offerings of pilgrims at the shrine of Thomas Cantelope enabled the canons to erect the central tower. The pinnacles are nineteenth-century additions.

The west front was destroyed by the fall of the western towers in the eighteenth century, the outcome of long neglect and ill-treatment by the Cromwellians. It was rebuilt in 1788 by Wyatt and is woefully out of keeping with the Romanesque style.

The handsome north porch was erected early in the sixteenth century and has a chapel above with Perpendicular-style windows. It leads to an inner porch of the thirteenth century.

INTERIOR

The nave arcades are Romanesque, dating from 1145, with the capitals increasingly decorated towards the east. Triforium and clerestory and plaster vaulting are the incongruous work of Wyatt in the eighteenth century.

The handsome font is twelfth century, and near it stands

the simple, movable pulpit from which a courageous dean rebuked the Cromwellian soldiers for their ill-treatment of the fabric. The alabaster effigy of a knight is late fourteenth century.

The north transept was built in the thirteenth century and holds what remains of the shrine of St. Thomas Cantelope: the sculptured base on which the reliquary was placed.

The builder of the transept, Bishop Aquablanca, rests in an ornate tomb at the entrance to the north ambulatory. Nearby is a unique thirteenth-century map of the world and, eastwards, the tomb and finely sculptured, fifteenth-century chantry chapel, with fan-vaulting and a tasteless reredos to the altar of modern design.

The early twelfth-century choir has a fine Romanesque triforium and a clerestory added a century later. The high altar stands picturesquely in a Norman arch backed by a decorated column. The richly carved cathedra, with chaplains' seats, and choir stalls, with fine misericords, are late fourteenth century.

North of the altar stands a chair reputedly used by King Stephen, and on the south is a defaced statue of the murdered Ethelbert whose brutal death is depicted on the paving.

Nave and choir are separated by Scott's ill-conceived screen, in the making of which he is said to have used 11,000 lb of iron, 5,000 lb of copper and 50,000 pieces of mosaic.

Eastwards stands the splendid thirteenth-century Lady Chapel, sheltering ornate tombs and a handsome fifteenth-century chantry. The modern reredos to the altar is of beautiful design.

The south transept is Romanesque with later, fan-vaulted roof.

The cloisters, entered by a doorway west of the transept, were restored in the fifteenth century and only a remnant of the Chapter House has survived. One arm of the fifteenth-century cloister of the vicars-choral adjoins the south choir ambulatory.

Despite the fact that two tons of ancient brasses were sold in 1786, several brasses remain *in situ*. But the cathedral's most precious possession is its medieval chained library of 5,000 books, a collection begun in early Norman times.

LEICESTER

The Church of St. Martin was raised to cathedral status on the formation of the diocese in 1926. Predominantly fifteenth century in origin, it has been much restored.

EXTERIOR

The tower, with broach spire, dates from 1867, replacing a Norman tower.

The handsome Vaughan Porch on the south was built thirty years later, with muniments room above, and has attractive statues.

The north porch has a fifteenth-century oaken roof.

INTERIOR

The thirteenth-century nave has a hammerbeam roof of last century with carved angels holding heraldic shields. The rood screen is modern and the pulpit has a seventeenth-century tester.

The north transept contains a small relic of the Norman church.

The choir was restored in the nineteenth century, a replica of its fifteenth-century predecessor. The east window has good modern glass and there is an attractive window dedicated to St. Dunstan in the south chapel. The western bays are occupied by a military chapel and the east by the chancellor's court—once the Lady Chapel, with grotesque corbel carvings.

LICHFIELD

In 669 Bishop Chad abdicated the Bishopric of York in favour of the irascible Wilfred and came south to Mercia.

Here he built a church at Stowe, on the far side of the pool adjacent to the present cathedral, and during his brief episcopate of three years earned for himself a reputation for saintliness. His body was encased in a wooden shrine shaped like a little house and the first cathedral was built in 700 to receive it.

In 786 the see was raised to an archbishopric, but for only seventeen years. Latterly it was merged with Chester and with Coventry and only last century was the present title adopted.

A new church was built for the saint's shrine in the twelfth century. The building suffered appalling damage at the hands of the Cromwellians who seized the Close in 1643; two thousand cannon shots and fifteen hundred grenades are said to have been fired against the fabric, the central tower battered down and the church left roofless and in ruins. Wyatt and Scott added ill-conceived restorations.

The bones of the saint now rest in Birmingham and no remnant of his shrine survives. But the cathedral library possesses one precious relic of Saxon times: the priceless Gospels of St. Chad.

EXTERIOR

The cathedral is best viewed from a distance from which the banality of the restored west front is not perceived. Built originally in 1293, it was drastically restored last century. Only five of the statues of the kings are original, the remainder being unworthy Victorian reproductions. Two pairs of the hinges of the central door are also originals.

This is the only English cathedral retaining its three spires, the western pair completed in 1320, but the central spire was demolished by the Roundheads' cannon and rebuilt at the end of the seventeenth century.

There are richly decorated doorways north and south; the former is said to have been dug out from accumulated soil in the last century.

INTERIOR

The nave was built in 1258, completing the rebuilding of the Norman cathedral which had been erected early in the previous century. It is separated from the choir by Scott's inadequate metal screen, replacing the original pulpitum.

The north transept is occupied by the Chapel of St. Stephen, of which the altar has an alabaster reredos.

The choir, standing on the same level as the nave, but at a noticeable angle to it, was the earliest part of the present church to be erected at the close of the twelfth century. The deflection of choir and nave was most probably dictated by the site. It is sometimes asserted that the design of the Gothic church is representative of the crucifixion, the transepts symbolizing Christ's outstretched arms and the deflected choir his bent head, but where such deflection occurs—as at Canterbury, Ely, York and here at Lichfield, it results from the builder's use of the site; the cruciform design of the church has no symbolic significance.

Stalls and cathedra were designed by Gilbert Scott in 1856. The high altar has candlesticks of the sixteenth century.

The shrine of St. Chad stood east of the high altar in the presbytery; it was the large number of pilgrims to this shrine which enabled the first Norman church to be rebuilt in the present form. Both presbytery and Lady Chapel belong to the early thirteenth century, while in 1225 the Chapel of St. Chad's Head was added south of the choir aisle, fronted by a gallery from which the relic was displayed.

There is an Epstein bust of Bishop Woods in the presbytery and the east windows of the Lady Chapel have sixteenth-century Flemish glass. Opposite the Chapel of St. Chad's Head is the tomb of Bishop Hacket, whose restoration of the church after the Civil War is recorded in stained glass.

The south transept has decorative bosses in the vaulting and an altar dedicated to St. Michael.

The Chapter House, with central column and canopied

stalls, was erected in 1249 and is approached by a cloister-like vestibule. This was the only part of the cathedral to retain its roof after the Cromwellian bombardment. The cathedral cat is carved on the bishop's chair, and St. Christopher, patron of travellers, presides over the vestibule.

LINCOLN

A cathedral is said to have been situated at nearby Stowe as early as the ninth century, but the bishopric was later transferred to Dorchester-on-Thames. After the Norman Conquest a bishop named Remigius was rewarded for his loyal support of William's cause by the presentation of the see. At Lincoln he found a Saxon community settled about a minster whose clergy acted as a group ministry to the surrounding villages. Remigius cleared the hilltop of home-steads and erected there the first church; built in the Romanesque style, it was consecrated shortly after his death, in 1092. Fifty years later fire consumed the wooden roof and hardly had it been replaced by a stone vault than the building was almost totally wrecked by an earthquake, only the western bay of the nave and façade escaping.

The famed St. Hugh was elected to the bishopric the following year, 1186, the see then having been vacant for nineteen years. He immediately set about raising money for its restoration and it was completed thirty-five years after his death, in 1235. However on his canonization in the same century the eastern chevet which he had built was demolished and replaced with a new choir with square termination, known as the Angel Choir, architecturally the cathedral's outstanding feature.

EXTERIOR

The western front is of much splendour, combining the deeply recessed doorways of Remigius's building with the Gothic curtain wall of St. Hugh. The remarkable panels depicting the sufferings of the damned are twelfth century. The small turrets either side bear sculptures of St. Hugh with his swan and the swineherd of Stowe who gave his life's savings to the building.

On the south side a thirteenth-century Galilee porch gives access to the transept, and a second porch of the same date, with sculpture of our Lord in judgement, is set between two later chantries and leads to the choir.

A sculpture of a pilgrim is set beneath the east window of the south-west tower and, farther east, there are contemporary statues of Edward I and his queen and a rich, thirteenth-century gable.

The central tower of the Norman building collapsed in 1237 and was replaced by the present splendid one in the following century. Originally it was topped by a wooden spire giving it greater height than any other in England, 524 ft., but the spire was blown down in 1584 and has never been replaced.

INTERIOR

The vestibule entrance stands below a Norman tower, but its walls have been wholly restored, two in 1280 and two in the eighteenth century.

The immense nave was erected in 1235, but the western termination retains a portion of the earlier church. The magnificent font is twelfth century.

The north transept has a splendid window of 1200 with its original glass, one panel depicting the burial of St. Hugh when his coffin was borne by the King of Scotland, King John and three archbishops. The transept has three chapels and remarkable architecture reflecting the experimental work of the builders.

The choir was completed prior to the nave in the late twelfth century, separated from it by a thirteenth-century stone screen with sculptures restored in the eighteenth century. The stalls are thirteenth century and have no less than one hundred original misericords of the total of seven hundred remaining in the cathedrals. Wren's reredos to the high altar is hardly in keeping.

North of the altar is an ornate Easter Sepulchre, with sleeping soldiers, in which the Blessed Sacrament was reserved from Maundy Thursday to Easter Day. A silver-gilt figure of Christ, with hollowed breast, served in medieval times as the aumbry.

Beyond the altar is the Angel Choir, 1260–80, with the famous Lincoln imp high on the north wall and the place of Hugh's burial marked on the paving. Of the golden coffin which held his body and the rich shrine there are no remains. As in the case of St. Chad at Lichfield, the saint's head was preserved in a separate reliquary of which the stone base is still to be seen. On the north is a fifteenth-century chantry and on the south two chantries of the sixteenth century. In the Middle Ages the church is reputed to have held thirty-six chantry altars.

The small transept was built in 1192. Westward, the south transept with its handsome window filled now with fragments of medieval glass, dates from the following century. Here rests the great Bishop Grosseteste, whose chalice is preserved in the Treasury with one of the few surviving copies of Magna Carta and the Conqueror's charter. The effigy of Bishop King is of splendid workmanship. The transept has three chapels, one with a charming St. Anne and another with a small, praying priest carved on the door jamb.

The cloisters, thirteenth century, with a north walk rebuilt by Wren and totally out of keeping, have an effigy of their designer, Richard of Gainsborough. The magnificent Chapter House was erected at the same date as the cloisters and has a central pillar circled by polished purbeck shafts, and arcaded seats.

LIVERPOOL

Old St. Paul's boasted a length of 526 ft.; the cathedral at Liverpool, designed by Sir Giles Gilbert Scott, when completed will be 636 ft. in length, making it one of the greatest churches in the world. At present, 100 ft. of the nave await completion.

Built of local sandstone on an imposing site, the foundation stone was laid in 1904 and the Lady Chapel completed six years later. Twice the work has been interrupted by war, and in the last war the south wall was damaged by a bomb and the Lady Chapel put out of use for fifteen years.

The diocese was formed in 1880.

EXTERIOR

The central Vestey tower, 347 ft. in height, is one of the great towers of the world, sheltering the heaviest peal of bells on earth.

On the south side the Rankin porch admits to the crossing and has effigies of King George V and Queen Mary, who waited here, arriving too early for the consecration. A beautifully carved panel depicts Christ and the children.

INTERIOR

Viewed from the west end of the uncompleted nave, it is apparent that the great church was designed primarily as a preaching house rather than for the celebration of the liturgy. Nave and choir are separated by a magnificent jube west of the crossing which provides an unrivalled view of crossing and choir.

The baptistry occupies the south-west transept, with dignified font sculptured with figures of the apostles beneath an elegant cover and oaken baldacchino.

In the choir is a handsome stone cathedra which, like the gilt-embellished reredos to the high altar, is an integral part of the fabric.

The Lady Chapel is at the eastern termination of the south choir aisle and is at a lower level than the main building. Galleries surmount the arcades and the altar has a reredos depicting the Nativity. The organ is above the broad western arch.

At the eastern termination of the north aisle is situated the Chapter House, with handsome doorway and the provision of an altar.

At the western end of the north choir aisle is the Chapel of the Holy Spirit, with an alabaster reredos depicting Christ at prayer and an almost life-size kneeling Madonna, the fifteenth-century work of della Robbia.

The cathedral boasts the highest traverse arches of any church.

By 1960 £2,500,000 had been spent on the building, the whole from public subscription and the munificent gifts of the Liverpool ship-owners.

LONDON: ST. PAUL'S

In the sixth century Pope Gregory had ordered Augustine to found an Archbishopric in London, but the hostility of the inhabitants prevented this. Nevertheless, Old St. Paul's occupied one of the most ancient Christian sites in the country. Itself among the greatest of Christian buildings, completed in 1315, it had become ruinous when the Great Fire devoured it. The history of its predecessors had also been disastrous. The first church was destroyed by fire in 675, its successor wrecked by Viking pirates, and the building of the choir in Norman times had been interrupted by fire. In 1447 the spire, the highest in Europe, was struck by lightning, and in the following century Lord Somerset demolished the cloisters to obtain stone for the building on his palace on the Embankment. The restoration of the building, begun in 1632, was interrupted by the Civil War and Cromwell adopted the church as a barracks. Christopher Wren, commissioned to restore the cathedral, after carting away forty-seven thousand cart-loads of rubbish, decided that he must build anew.

Wren's cathedral was intended to be the centre-piece of a redesigned London, all its roads converging upon a vast square dominated by the church, surrounded by triumphal archways and spacious streets. Constantly frustrated by his superiors and those who had financial interests in the remaining properties, Wren's church alone materialized and even that bore little resemblance to the agreed design.

Even in the building of it the frustrations continued. When members of the Royal Academy offered to fill the compartments of the archways with pictures the Archbishop of Canterbury cried 'Popery!', and the high altar had to wait two hundred and fifty years for its baldacchino. In 1711 the architect was forced to petition the queen to obtain his pay.

EXTERIOR

The west front dominates the approach from Ludgate Hill, with double portico and pillared towers flanking the Grecian columns.

The mighty dome, topped by the glittering cross, is formed of a stone cone covered by an outer dome of wood with a skin of lead.

The figure of St. Paul stands above the tympanum which depicts his conversion. The clock has a diameter of nearly 19 ft. and an 8-ft. minute hand weighing 75 lb. The great eighteenth-century bell which strikes the hours weighs nearly four tons.

INTERIOR

From the western end there is an uninterrupted view to the high altar, Wren's organ screen, which originally stood west of the crossing, having been removed in the nineteenth century. Flanked by arcades of coffered arches upheld by huge piers, the vaulting is shallow-domed, the choir enriched with

gilding and the high altar is beneath a magnificent baldacchino of the present century, replacing bomb damage in the
last war. Choir stalls are by Grinling Gibbons and the aisles
closed by Jean Tijou's handsome wrought-iron gates, while
screens by the same artist flank the sanctuary.

The interior brick dome has eighteenth-century frescoes.

The western bay of the nave is flanked by chapels; the
northern of these, dedicated to St. Dunstan, is of entrancing
beauty. There is a massive memorial to the Duke of Welling-
ton and, in the south aisle, Holman Hunt's 'Light of the
World'.

The eighteenth-century bird-bath font stands in the south
transept. Farther east, in the choir aisle, is the shrouded
effigy of Dr. John Donne; this is the sole surviving relic of the
old cathedral, and there is no trace of the once-famed shrine
of St. Erkenwald, goal of countless medieval pilgrims. The
choir aisle is terminated by a charming Lady Chapel, which
has a lovely Madonna by Josepha da Vasconcellas.

East of the high altar a chapel is dedicated to those Ameri-
cans who, based in the United Kingdom, died in the last war.

The dismal atmosphere of the crypt, the largest in Europe,
is relieved by the handsome Chapel of the Order of the
British Empire at its eastern end. Nelson is buried here in a
sixteenth-century sarcophagus intended for Cardinal Wolsey,
but the most touching memorial is the plain grave of Wren
himself, inscribed *Si monumentum requiris, circumspice* (If you
seek his monument, look around you).

MANCHESTER

Although the Bishopric of Manchester dates only from
1847, the site of the cathedral is an ancient one, once most
probably that of a Saxon church. But the present church
enters history in 1398 when a priest inherited the local manor,
made it into a community house for eight priests and was
granted a charter allowing him to build the church. The

existing building has, however, seen such drastic restoration that little of the fourteenth-century fabric remains.

EXTERIOR

The western tower was rebuilt in 1867, when the original tower was in a ruinous and dangerous condition.

Both north and south porches were rebuilt in the last century, both with modern sculptures, by Eric Gill and Alan Durst respectively.

INTERIOR

The western tower arch is a relic of the fourteenth-century building, but the fifteenth-century nave and aisles were so weakened by 'improvements' of 1815 that it had to be largely replaced in 1882 when new work was closely modelled on the old.

The clerestory windows of the nave had been added at the close of the fifteenth century, and in the same century the windows of the nave aisles were removed to allow the erection of additional aisles north and south for the provision of chantry chapels. Until last century the wooden screens dividing these chapels were in place; by their demolition to provide room for larger congregations the church is now possessed of double aisles, making it one of the widest in the country.

The handsome nave roof is modern, with corbel angels and finely carved bosses.

The restored wooden pulpitum has survived from medieval times, with painted panelling and a nineteenth-century cornice.

The choir was built at the end of the fifteenth century by Bishop Stanley, whose body is reputed to have been exhumed last century and found to have a height of 6 ft. 4 in. 'A goodlie tall man as was in all England and spedd well in all matters that he took in hand.'

Once there were statues of the Virgin Mary and St. Denis

on pillars adjoining the choir and 'unto them men did usually bow on their coming into the church'. The stalls, though much defaced and restored, have fine carving of 1508 not least in their misericords. The parclose screens in the eastern bays are early sixteenth century, but much defaced by seventeenth-century alterations to them. A beautiful sixteenth-century screen separates the southern chapel.

The termination of the northern aisle is occupied by a regimental chapel, a restoration after bomb damage in the last war of a sixteenth-century chapel.

The Lady Chapel has been rebuilt after bomb damage, but the screen, which escaped, is of the sixteenth century. The bronze Madonna by Sir Charles Wheeler wears the dress of a Lancashire mill girl, and a delightful modern tapestry depicts the Annunciation.

The attractive fan-vaulting at the crossing was added in 1867 when the tower was rebuilt.

A marble statue commemorates Humphrey Chetham, who founded the adjacent school in the sixteenth century, and a fifteenth-century brass remembers John Huntington, first warden of the priests' college. On exhibition are the Saxon stone found on the site, and the charter of Henry V.

NEWCASTLE

Although Edward VI proposed the founding of a bishopric at Newcastle the see was not formed until 1878. The church chosen to be the cathedral is among the largest parish churches in England.

The first church on the site was erected in 1091 and destroyed by fire in 1216. The present building, largely thirteenth-century, was saved from destruction by the Scots when a resourceful mayor confined his Scottish prisoners in the belfry, but Puritans smashed the ancient glass. In 1784 the medieval brasses were sold by auction.

EXTERIOR

The fifteenth-century lantern tower of unusual and delicate design, the steeple upheld by a crown of flying buttresses, is an outstanding feature of the church.

INTERIOR

The nave was built in 1350 and has the peculiarity of being narrower than its aisles, possibly on account of the eighteen chantry chapels which the church once boasted. The handsome fifteenth-century font has blue and gold shields and a medieval cover. The pre-Reformation eagle lectern is a rarity.

The choir, built in 1368, is separated by a modern screen, and the reredos of the high altar has figures of St. Cuthbert and St. Wilfred. Beyond it, three chapels with modern stained glass in their windows occupy the eastern wall.

The south transept shelters a fourteenth-century effigy of a knight and, westward, a chapel dedicated to St. Margaret of Scotland has a Madonna in medieval glass. In the fourteenth-century crypt, once an ossuary attached to a chantry chapel above, is now the Chapel of the Blessed Sacrament.

NORWICH

Norwich was once in the Saxon see of East Anglia, with its cathedral—doubtless of wood—at Dunwich. Later the see was divided and a cathedral built at North Elmham in 673, the first wooden building being replaced by one of stone in the following century. This was burned by the Danes in 870 and left in ruins until rebuilt in 950. But with the coming of the Normans the see was moved to the more populated centre of Thetford and later to Norwich, where the present church was built in 1095.

The builder was Bishop Herbert de Losinga, reputed to have bribed William Rufus to elect him to the bishopric and then, repenting, to have raised the present cathedral as his penance.

EXTERIOR

At the west end the doorway is early fifteenth century and the window above it was inserted in 1470.

The tower is twelfth century, the lower portion being completed before Bishop Losinga's death in 1119. The original spire was blown down in a gale in 1362 and its successor struck by lightning almost exactly a century later. The present spire was built at the close of the fifteenth century.

Over the north transept door is an ancient image which may be that of Bishop Losinga.

The flying buttresses supporting the clerestory of the choir are fourteenth century.

Three of the monastic gateways remain: the Erpingham Gate, 1420, admitted to the cathedral precincts; the Ethelbert Gate, south-west, admitted to the monastery grounds; the Water Gate is adjacent to the river, eastwards.

INTERIOR

The Norman nave was completed before 1145, but the lierne vault was added in 1470 at the same time as the insertion of the west window.

The pulpitum was built in 1465.

Both transepts are twelfth century and have their early sixteenth-century vaults and ornate roof bosses. In the north transept St. Andrew's Chapel has a thirteenth-century window, with glass of the sixteenth century, and a modern Madonna.

The choir stalls date back to 1420 with fine misericords, and there is a fourteenth-century lectern. The presbytery is unique in retaining its apsidal termination. The clerestory and vault were damaged by the fall of the spire in 1362 and the present lierne vault was built by Bishop Goldwell at the end of the fifteenth century, the clerestory windows having been

G

restored by his predecessor. Bishop Losinga is buried before the high altar, and the fine effigy of Bishop Goldwell is on the south side of the presbytery; his rebus should be noted.

North of the presbytery the Erpingham window has medieval glass.

The ancient episcopal throne, raised on steps behind the altar, is the most precious possession of the cathedral, incorporating Saxon stones of the original cathedral situated at Dunwich and subsequently re-erected both at North Elmham and at Thetford. This is the only English cathedral having its cathedra positioned east of the altar.

In the ambulatory is a fifteenth-century font depicting the seven sacraments, and a low 'reliquary arch' of 1424 that once gave access to a reliquary chapel. A thirteenth-century doorway admits to St. Saviour's Chapel at the eastern termination, on the site of the first Lady Chapel. The altar has a magnificent fourteenth-century retable with painted panels. On the north, the Jesus Chapel dates from 1096, as does St. Luke's Chapel on the south.

The south walk of the ambulatory leads to the Bauchon Chapel built in 1330, with ornate roof bosses.

The cloisters were rebuilt after destruction by rioters between 1297 and 1430, the north walk being the last to be raised, and they are perhaps the finest Norman work in the country. Benches scratched with the play-boards of novices' games and the lavatorium remain, while the vaulting is magnificently decorated with sculptured bosses, all with their colour restored, depicting Biblical scenes.

Apart from the ruins of the refectory and doorways which once led to the various domestic rooms of the monastery, little else remains.

OXFORD

In 730 a petty king named Didanus built at Oxford a church in memory of his wife. His daughter, Frideswide, who was betrothed to a local king, was determined to take the veil of a nun and fled here to escape him.

Didanus founded a nunnery for his daughter and this was rebuilt by the Normans in 1122. At the dissolution Henry VIII presented church and endowments to his favourite, Wolsey, who proceeded to demolish the cloisters and western bays of the nave to obtain stone for the building of Christ Church college. The total destruction of the church was prevented only by his fall from grace. The church now fulfils the dual role of cathedral and college chapel.

EXTERIOR

The spire was built in the thirteenth century and is reputed to be the oldest spire in the country.

At the east end of the church three arches, once part of the Saxon church, have been built into the fabric.

INTERIOR

The nave arcades, dating from the twelfth century, are of unique design, but the north nave aisle is fifteenth century.

The choir, with fine fan-vaulting, is late fifteenth century and has stalls of the same date.

The church is unique in retaining five Norman vaults, including that of the sacristy. The timbered roof of the nave is sixteenth century and that of the lantern seventeenth century.

The Lady Chapel is thirteenth century and the Latin and St. Lucy Chapels are fourteenth century. The windows of the Latin Chapel contain fourteenth-century glass as well as that of the seventeenth century. Several of the cathedral windows are by Burne-Jones (1833–98).

Behind the choir stalls are finely wrought iron screens. The base of St. Frideswide's shrine, made in 1289 and displaying the earliest known leaf sculpture, stands in the north choir aisle. Nearby is the fifteenth-century wooden watching chamber, one of the only two remaining examples, with chantry chapel beneath.

The south aisle of the nave gives access to the partially demolished cloisters where a fifteenth-century doorway admits to the sacristy and a Norman doorway to the Chapter House. The fifteenth-century cloisters have modern vaulting, but retain the contemporary bosses.

The Chapter House is an outstanding example of thirteenth-century architecture, with lancet windows, arcaded walls and finely sculptured capitals. The windows contain glass of the seventeenth century.

The church has brasses of the fifteenth, sixteenth and seventeenth centuries and the tomb of a fourteenth-century prior.

PETERBOROUGH

The first abbey is reputed to have been planned by Peada, King of the Mercians, in the seventh century, but he was assassinated before he could begin the work. Later his brother, Wulfhere, who had slain his two sons for adopting the Christian Faith, was brought to repentance by St. Chad and ordered to build the abbey as his penance. On its completion it was dedicated to St. Peter, and the town, previously known as Medeshamsted, renamed Peterborough.

In 870 the church was burned by the Danes and the monks murdered. For a hundred years it remained in ruins until rebuilt in 972 by Aethelwold, Bishop of Winchester, in obedience to a vision. The following century it was burned by Hereward the Wake in protest at the appointment of a Norman abbot, and finally rebuilt—largely in its present form—in 1192. On its surrender at the dissolution it was made a cathedral, the last abbot becoming the first bishop.

Much damage was done to the fabric and furnishings by the Cromwellians, and it was not until last century that it was restored.

EXTERIOR

The west front, possibly the most splendid example of late Romanesque architecture in the country, was built in 1237, with flanking towers to act as buttresses. At the end of the fourteenth century a porchway was added to the central arch. The west doors are of medieval wood.

The central tower became unsafe in the thirteenth century, the present tower, with incongruous pinnacles, dating from 1884.

The statues in the façade are modern restorations by Alan Durst.

A subway beneath the south transept allows a view of the foundations of the Saxon church, and the foundations of the demolished Lady Chapel, sold to provide funds for eighteenth-century restorations, are to be seen north of choir.

INTERIOR

The magnificent Romanesque nave was built in 1220 and retains its original wooden vault, the colouring restored. The Perpendicular windows in the nave aisles, however, were inserted in the fifteenth century.

The font has a thirteenth-century bowl on a modern base.

Either side of the west doors are mural paintings, recently discovered, executed at the end of the sixteenth century and depicting the sexton who buried both Katherine of Aragon and Mary, Queen of Scots. Both queens had graves in the cathedral, though Mary's body was moved to London by her son.

The crossing has pointed arches east and west and was rebuilt and strengthened in 1887. The original pulpitum no longer exists and the view to the high altar is unimpeded.

The choir's ceiling is richly ornamented. The stalls are nineteenth century, with carvings either side depicting the vision of Aethelwold and the story of King Oswald. The latter's arm was a relic preserved by the monastery. The lectern is fifteenth century. The windows of the apse behind the high altar have fourteenth-century tracery and some medieval glass.

The eastern extension was added shortly before the dissolution, early in the sixteenth century. The medieval painted shields on the apse pillars and the inscribed names of three archbishops buried in the church should be noted, also Abbot Kirkton's rebus.

South-east of the sanctuary is the Saxon monks' stone which may date from the eighth century. On the north side is the fifteenth-century restored base of a shrine once dedicated to a St. Tibba, a Saxon lady, while the south transept has a modern chapel to St. Oswald and the remnant of a stairway once giving access to a watching chamber from which guard was kept over the relics of the saint.

The domestic buildings of the monastery survive only by fragmentary remains: an arcade of the infirmary now forming the south wall of the cloisters, a sixteenth-century oriel window with Abbot Kirkton's rebus below, a gateway, the little dorter once attached to the infirmary and a Tudor archway known as the Prior's Gate, with the sculptured arms of King Edmund of East Anglia.

PORTSMOUTH

The first church was built at the end of the twelfth century, dedicated to St. Thomas à Becket and given into the charge of Augustinian Canons. Its tower was used as a naval watchtower, but suffered heavy damage during the Civil War and both nave and tower were subsequently rebuilt.

The church became the cathedral of the new diocese in 1927 and ambitious plans to enlarge it have since been only partially executed.

EXTERIOR

The tower dates from 1691. The cupola was added in 1703. The weathervane is modern.

INTERIOR

The nave, built in this century, is incomplete and will eventually have four further bays. At the west end may be seen the foundation stone, laid by Lord Montgomery in 1944. Also displayed is the weathervane barque which for 250 years stood on the apex of the cupola. In the south aisle is a fragment of the flag of Nelson's *Victory*, and there are other mementoes of the cathedral's long association with the Royal Navy.

A low jube is modern, joining the new building to the gallery of 1708. The organ case was made in 1718.

North of the crossing a sixteenth-century font stands in the baptistry, and there is a della Robbia Madonna of 1500.

The choir, built in 1693, formed the nave of the eighteenth-century church. The pulpit, with its trumpeting angel, was made in 1694. The Corporation pew is of the same date.

The north sanctuary aisle has unusual vaulting and leads into the Lady Chapel, which belongs to the earliest church, built in 1196. The sanctuary and Martyrs' Chapel on the south are also twelfth century. The varied designs of the transept windows, all of similar date, should be noted.

RIPON

A Saxon monastery was founded here in the seventh century, and shortly afterwards St. Wilfred built a stone church of which the crypt survives. This was burned by the Danes in the ninth century, but apparently rebuilt, as in 934 it was declared one of the sanctuary churches. After William the Conqueror's brutal devastation of the north it remained a ruin until rebuilt in 1080. Latterly it suffered from the vandalism of the Scots in the fourteenth century and the Cromwellians, who three hundred years later smashed all the ancient glass. In 1604 James I had re-established the Chapter and placed the church in the care of dean and canons. It was adopted as the cathedral of the new diocese in 1836.

EXTERIOR

The south door survives from the church building of the latter half of the twelfth century.

The west front was built in 1220. All three towers were topped by wooden spires. Part of the central tower collapsed in 1450 and, though its rebuilding was begun forty years later when the nave was enlarged, it was not completed. The spire of the central tower fell in 1660 and four years afterwards the western spires were removed for fear of similar calamities.

The western entrance has seventeenth-century oaken doors.

INTERIOR

The west window was built in the mid-thirteenth century. Two western bays of the nave are of the same date, but the eastern bays, together with the nave aisles, belong to the enlargements of the early sixteenth century, as do the generous clerestory windows.

The magnificent pulpitum dividing nave from choir was built in 1500. The coloured statuary has been restored in the present century, bringing back to the church some of the brilliant colouring of medieval times.

The thirteenth-century north transept displays both the rounded and the pointed arch. Near its entrance stands a stone pulpit of Perpendicular design which once stood on the pulpitum.

The crossing is remarkable for possessing two arches of the earlier church of the twelfth century and two of the fifteenth century when extensive rebuilding was undertaken. The attractive metal and marble pulpit, made at the beginning of the present century, has figures of Saxon saints.

The choir is dominated by the great east window of 1286. The glass is nineteenth century. The south side of the choir shows architecture both of the late thirteenth century and the sixteenth. The roof bosses survive from the earlier building, replaced by Scott in his nineteenth-century vault. The stalls were made at the end of the fifteenth century and have delightful misericords and handsomely carved finials and canopies.

The high altar is flanked by coloured statues of St. Peter and St. Wilfred. The shrine of the latter once stood at the east end of the church, attracting numerous pilgrims.

The Chapter House, once part of the Norman church, has an altar in its eleventh-century apsidal east end; the undercroft also survives from the Norman church. The library, once the Lady Chapel, was built above the present Chapter House at the end of the fourteenth century. A stairway leads into the south transept; one wall retains mural painting of the twelfth century.

The windows of the south side aisle preserve fragments of medieval glass. A tomb once ornamented by a brass depicting a lion among trees is of fourteenth-century workmanship.

On the south side of the crossing is the entrance to the cramped and ancient crypt which was part of the seventh-century church built by Wilfred.

ROCHESTER

The cathedral was founded by St. Augustine in 604. Its site near the river made it an inevitable target for Danish raids, and the Normans found it in a ruinous condition. Bishop Gundulph rebuilt the church in 1080, but it was much damaged by fires in the following century. The fourteenth-century rebuilding was partially financed by the offerings of pilgrims at the shrine of St. William of Perth who, though never canonized, was popularized as a local saint, but the completion of this rebuilding was prevented by lack of funds. The church suffered from the vandalism of the Puritans, but most of all at the hands of eighteenth- and nineteenth-century restorers.

EXTERIOR

The west front is Romanesque dating, as does the ornately sculptured western entrance, from 1130. The flanking statues of Henry I and his queen are reputedly the oldest in the country.

The towers originally carried pill-box terminations, but the outer ones were destroyed in 1793 and the restorations date from 1888; only the pinnacle of the south tower is original. The central tower fell in 1343 and since then has been frequently rebuilt, last in 1904.

On the north side of the church the tower between the two transepts, built in 1080, probably as a refuge from raiders, survives.

The arcading of the cloisters, built in 1125 and destroyed by fire, may be seen south of the choir.

INTERIOR

The west window was inserted in 1470.

The nave is the oldest in England, dating from the late eleventh and early twelfth centuries. The triforium has the earliest pointed arches in the country. The clerestory was added in the fifteenth century. A mural painting representing St. Christopher is to be seen on a southern pillar. At the east end of the nave the conjoining of work of 1300 with the earlier arcade marks the point at which finances prevented further rebuilding.

The aisle pillars were refaced in the twelfth century, though the south face of those of the south aisle have not been altered.

The Lady Chapel was added south of the nave in 1490.

The north transept was built in the mid-thirteenth century, the south some thirty years later.

The fourteenth-century pulpitum has statues of 1880.

The choir was built in 1227, the lower, solid walls of the earlier building being retained. The mural decoration of the fourteenth century has been restored; on the northern side is painted a medieval 'Wheel of Fortune'.

Two effigies of bishops, thirteenth and fourteenth century respectively, are situated east of the choir. Bishop Gundulph is buried near the high altar. The reredos of the altar is an incongruous addition by Scott in the last century.

A plain slab of stone lying in the presbytery is the sole relic of the shrine of St. William which once stood in the choir transept. He was a baker of Perth who in 1201 made a pilgrimage to Becket's shrine at Canterbury, staying at the Rochester monastery en route. The following morning he was murdered by his servant and his body discovered under a hedge. He was buried in the church and, though his canonization was refused, the monks succeeded in popularizing him as a saint and thereby attracted considerable revenue to their monastery.

In the south transept is a door of 1340 admitting to the Chapter Room; the settlement of the columns is to be noted.

The south choir aisle has a medieval wooden vestry.

The crypt belongs partially to Gundulph's church, the western end dating from 1080; there are three altars in the thirteenth-century eastern end and on the piers are some medieval graffiti.

SAINT ALBANS

Alban is the first name of a martyred English Christian, who may have suffered execution as early as 209. He is reputed to have been an officer in the Roman army who gave refuge to a Christian priest and took his place to enable him to escape. A church was built on the crown of the hill where he died, probably within a few years of his death. Both Gildas writing in 550, and Bede writing in 730, mention the church.

The abbey was founded in 793, rebuilt by the Normans and re-dedicated in 1115, subsequently becoming the richest monastic house in the country. At the dissolution the church was sold to the townspeople for £400 and, though Henry VIII proposed that it should become the cathedral of a new diocese, it was not raised to that status until 1877.

EXTERIOR

The central tower was built of Roman bricks from the ruins of nearby Verulamium. The west end collapsed in 1323 and the flanking towers were demolished to provide stone for rebuilding. When last century it was in a ruinous condition a wealthy benefactor, Lord Grimthorpe, carried out extensive restorations, including the rebuilding of the west front. The St. Matthew sculpture in the porch is his portrait.

The only remains of the domestic buildings of this once wealthy and powerful abbey are the arcading of the north wall of the cloister and the massive fourteenth-century gateway which until last century was used as a prison.

INTERIOR

The west window is nineteenth century.

The western bays, triforium and clerestory on the north side were built in 1210, joining the eleventh-century wall, with its severe arcade, triforium and clerestory. Five bays of the south arcade collapsed in 1323 and were rebuilt in that century. The portrait sculptures between the triforium arches should be noted, also the thirteenth- and fourteenth-century murals on the Norman pier faces, probably once forming the reredoses of altars.

The pulpitum, since robbed of its statues, was built in 1350 and possesses its original doors.

The crossing belongs to the Romanesque church of the eleventh century. Both transepts are defaced by nineteenth-century windows. The triforium in the south transept has Saxon columns saved from the pre-Norman church.

The presbytery, with a thirteenth-century wooden vault, is walled in by solid Norman masonry.

The altar is backed by a high reredos made in 1484, with restored statues. On the north side is the Ramryge Chantry, with ornate vaulting, built in 1521, the rebus of the bishop incorporated in the sculptured decoration. On the south is the magnificent brass of Bishop Thomas de la Mare, 1360.

The base of St. Alban's shrine was recovered last century from the rubble filling the eastern arches of the presbytery; it was reassembled from 2,000 fragments, and though only partially rebuilt, provides an impression of its appearance in medieval times. Then, before the erection of the altar reredos in the fifteenth century, the reliquary, brilliant with jewels and precious metals, could be seen above and beyond the altar, raised on its painted stone pedestal. The preserved base is carved with scenes of the martyrdom and still retains traces of medieval colouring. North of the shrine stands the watching chamber of 1400, with cupboards for relics beneath, from which monks kept sentinel as the streams of pilgrims walked in procession past the shrine. The woodwork has delightful carvings.

The eastern arcading bears a medieval mural painting of a twelfth-century archbishop, and to the south is the richly sculptured tomb of Humphrey of Gloucester, with thirteenth-century wrought-iron screens.

At the eastern termination of the building is the Lady Chapel erected in the early fourteenth century, with rich tracery in the eastern window and small, contemporary effigies either side. Vault and blind arcading are nineteenth century.

The base of St. Amphibulus' shrine is also preserved. Of somewhat doubtful authenticity, he was supposedly a priest whom St. Alban rescued and who fled to Wales.

SALISBURY

North of the present city of Salisbury the ruins of Old Sarum occupy a hilltop, consisting mainly of castle walls and the foundations of its cathedral. This latter was built within the castle walls by Bishop Osmund, who arrived with the Conqueror and was Chancellor of the realm.

His church was consecrated in 1092, but almost immediately damaged by lightning. The site proved unsatisfactory, for the howling of the wind interfered with the services, the clergy suffered from rheumatism and the soldiers at the castle sometimes made it difficult for people to obtain access to the cathedral. In 1217 Bishop Richard Poore petitioned the pope to rebuild it in the valley.

The new cathedral was begun in 1220 and completed forty-eight years later. The body of Osmund was moved to the new building, attracting pilgrims even though he was not officially canonized until the fifteenth century. The church was in the charge of secular canons, as Osmund had originally decreed, and gained fame for the orderliness and beauty of its liturgy.

EXTERIOR

The west front, like all the cathedral except the tower, was completed in 1265; the many statues do not merit close inspection. A detached bell-tower was demolished by Wyatt in the eighteenth century in a scheme of ruthless restoration. In the thirteenth century the central tower was squat, barely rising above the ridges of the roofs. Two additional stages and the magnificent spire were added in 1334. The spire, 404 ft. in height, preserves within it the medieval scaffolding and a fragment of the Virgin's gown in a leaden box. Flying buttresses to give additional support were added in the fifteenth century.

The setting of the cathedral and that of its close, walled in 1333 with stones brought from Old Sarum, make a picture of quiet charm. Richard Poore's hall is incorporated in the cathedral school buildings and there are houses of the seventeenth and eighteenth century. The buildings of the Hospital of St. Nicholas, erected in the early thirteenth century, are used as almshouses. The adjacent bridge was built in 1245.

INTERIOR

The entire interior of the cathedral belongs to the thirteenth century and thus possesses a rare harmony.

Little of the ancient glass has survived, but fragments are preserved in the west window.

In the nave is the effigy of a thirteenth-century knight by whose head the small stone sculptured with the figure of a bishop may have indicated the burial place of Richard Poore's heart. The only remnant of the once-revered shrine of Osmund is the ugly base stone. In the north aisle are the works of what may well be the oldest clock in England.

The east column of the north arcade shows signs of settlement beneath the weight of the tower. Additional arches were added at the entrance of the transepts in the fifteenth century. The vault of the tower is ornamented with lierne ribs. Inverted arches in the choir transepts, built in the late fourteenth century, were inserted to strengthen the walls against the outward thrust of the tower. The arcading in the north choir transept belonged to the medieval pulpitum which originally separated nave and choir and was removed by Wyatt. The choir stalls have modern canopies, but retain their thirteenth-century seats.

The whole church was dedicated to the Virgin, and the chapel at the east end to the Blessed Trinity. This was the first portion of the building to be completed, being dedicated in 1225. To the north stands an ornately sculptured monument of 1635 and, to the south, the stone of 1099 which once covered Osmund's grave.

The cloisters were the last portion of the original building to be built, in 1270, and are the largest and earliest in the country, though strictly out of place since the church has never been monastic. The library over the eastern wing was added in 1445, and the Chapter House, much damaged by Cromwell, in 1280. A shafted column of great delicacy supports the vault of the latter and beneath the windows a sculptured frieze depicts Biblical scenes. It contains a table of the thirteenth century. A number of side altars have been colourfully restored.

SHEFFIELD

The cathedral occupies the site of a church founded in the reign of Henry I, but during the eighteenth century the building was so neglected that it became an almost total ruin and in 1805 was wholly reconstructed. The present century has seen much enlargement of the building, into a light and spacious cathedral of great attraction.

The oaken sedilia of the fifteenth century is the sole link with the original building. The nave, with aisles, and clerestory without triforium, as well as the transepts, were built in the last century.

On the north side a lantern has been built. Steps lead to a handsome regimental chapel where colourful figures of St. George and St. Michael guard the approach and St. Martin and St. Oswald flank the altar. A crypt chapel beneath—actually on a level with the street—is dedicated to the Holy Spirit and has a beautiful little altar and Christ and the Apostles depicted on its painted reredos. Gilded angels decorate the doorway leading to offices.

The modern gilded cathedra has a figure of Christ. The vaulting is embellished with gilded angels and bosses. Altars stand north and south, and there is a Tudor memorial to an Earl of Shrewsbury.

SOUTHWARK

The site was occupied by a monastery in the reign of Edward the Confessor, but in 1106 a new church was built which was re-dedicated seventy years later to Thomas à Becket after his murder at Canterbury. Fire destroyed this building in 1212 and rebuilding was begun in the middle of that century but not completed until about 1310. Fire again damaged the church in 1385 and the fifteenth century saw further restoration, including the heightening of the central tower. At the dissolution of the monasteries it became a parish church and in 1614 was purchased by the parishioners. In the eighteenth century it fell into disrepair, two of its chapels were demolished and in the following century the nave was left roofless. Barely saved from demolition, the church received a new nave in 1890 and was adopted as the cathedral of the recently formed diocese in 1905.

EXTERIOR

The pinnacles of the thirteenth-century tower were added in 1689.

INTERIOR

The nave was rebuilt at the end of the last century. Bosses from the fifteenth-century wooden vaulting are seen at the west end where, on the north side, remnants of the thirteenth-century arcading survive.

A twelfth-century doorway in the north aisle once led to the cloisters and in the same aisle is the colourful tabernacle tomb of John Gower, 1408. Opposite, in the south aisle, a modern effigy beneath a window of great charm commemorates Shakespeare, whose Globe Theatre was nearby and whose younger brother, Edmund, was buried in the church.

A north transept chapel is in memory of John Harvard who, in 1638, emigrated to America and founded there the university which bears his name. In the south transept the arms of Cardinal Beaufort commemorate his rebuilding of the transept in 1420.

The piers of the crossing are thirteenth century, partially refaced the following century.

In the north choir aisle the wooden effigy of a knight dates from the early fourteenth century and two monuments are early seventeenth century. Bishop Lancelot Andrewes' tomb, moved last century from a chapel now demolished, stands south of the altar.

H

The magnificent stone screen behind the high altar was built in 1520 but the figures are modern.

The retrochoir, built in the thirteenth century, is a restoration. At its termination four chapels have colourful altars and graceful separating screens.

SOUTHWELL

The minster became the cathedral of the newly formed diocese in 1884.

EXTERIOR

The archway of the entrance gate is Norman, with later additions of gable and niche. The western and central towers were erected early in the twelfth century.

There are richly sculptured doorways north and south, the former two-storied. The western doors, framed in a Romanesque doorway, embody fine medieval ironwork.

The exterior of the church is richly ornamented with arcading and sculptured heads and gargoyles, particularly the thirteenth-century choir and Chapter House.

INTERIOR

The west window and those of the aisles date from the fifteenth century.

The nave was begun in 1110. The roof is nineteenth century, but aisles and twelfth-century transepts have their original Norman vaulting. The arches of the crossing are also twelfth century; the capitals of the eastern arch are carved with Scriptural scenes.

The doorway of the north transept has a Saxon tympanum. A fragment of Roman paving is to be seen beneath a trapdoor in the floor of the south transept.

The screen dividing nave from choir was made in 1330 and has no rival in England. The centre doorway is presided over by a Madonna and Child and on either side of the screen are nearly three hundred sculptured heads and figures: Biblical scenes, kings, knights and bishops. The attached stalls have canopies delicately sculptured with leaves. The wrought-iron gates are modern.

The choir is early fourteenth century, with Flemish glass in its eastern lancets and choir stalls of successful nineteenth-century carving, displaying leaves and flowers and animals. In the south choir aisle, where lies the twelfth-century effigy of a priest, the east window is filled with fragments of medieval glass. Other windows contain stained glass by Christopher Whall. The carved panel of an altar in a side chapel is fourteenth century.

The north choir aisle gives access to the Chapter House and its vestibule through a delicately sculptured doorway, with slender, shafted trumeau, the recessed arch ornamented with leaf carving of particular beauty.

Vestibule and Chapter House were built at the close of the thirteenth century. The walls have arcaded seats with intricately sculptured canopies.

Among the furnishings of the cathedral is a medieval eagle lectern rescued from a pond in the last century and once the property of Newstead Priory.

TRURO

In Saxon times Cornwall had a cathedral at St. Germains, but Edward the Confessor united the diocese to that of Exeter.

The present diocese was formed in 1887 and the foundation stone of the cathedral laid three years later. The church was completed in 1910, but had been consecrated while still unfinished. Its style is imitative Gothic, more suited to the Middle Ages than to the twentieth century.

The north aisle belonged to the sixteenth-century Church of St. Mary of which it is the only remaining part.

The south aisle baptistry of delicate columns, beautifully designed, is in memory of Henry Martyn, the pioneer missionary to Persia whose life is recalled in the baptistry windows.

Stained glass tells the story of the English Church and depicts the industries of Cornwall. The high altar has a handsome reredos of Cornish stone and an attractive sedilia.

A Chapter House of entirely different design has been added in this century.

Apart from the rebuilding of St. Paul's, this was the first cathedral to be erected since the Reformation. Designed by John L. Pearson, it was completed after his death by his son, F. L. Pearson. The Holy Communion has been offered daily within it without lapse since 1887.

WAKEFIELD

There was a Saxon church on this site of which a Saxon cross of 960, now in a York museum, may be the sole relic. This church was mentioned in Doomsday Book and was replaced by a second church in the twelfth century. Two hundred years later part of the building was demolished by the fall of the central tower; the new church was consecrated in 1329. In the following century the nave was lengthened and a tower added. In the fifteenth century a clerestory was added to the nave and the choir again rebuilt and the nave aisles enlarged. The church was further extended eastwards at the beginning of the present century, having been adopted as the cathedral of the new diocese in 1887.

EXTERIOR

The tower, with crocketted spire, was erected in the fifteenth century.

INTERIOR

The lower portions of two pillars on the north side of the nave are relics of the twelfth-century church, while the bases of columns on the south side are thirteenth century.

The chancel arch and nave arcading is fourteenth century. The screen is fifteenth century, with upper portion added in 1635 and a handsome modern rood. Font cover and pulpit are early eighteenth century. The south transept displays a replica of the Saxon cross.

WELLS

The diocese was founded in 909 and its first cathedral dedicated to St. Andrew, but with the coming of the Normans began two centuries of troubled history.

In 1088 the buildings were allowed to become ruinous when Bishop de Villula removed his see to Bath. A compromise attempted in 1136 when Bath and Wells were united, both churches housing the cathedra of the bishop, survived only until 1192 when Bishop Savaric assumed the title of Bishop of Bath and Glastonbury. His successor retained only the title of Bishop of Bath. Finally, the pope decreed in 1244 that the see should be that of Bath and Wells, and this title has been retained ever since, although the cathedra belongs exclusively to Wells.

The earliest church was built probably in 705, succeeded by new buildings in 1148 and 1184. The fabric was damaged by an earthquake in 1248.

EXTERIOR

The west front, dating from 1239, is among the most magnificent architectural achievements of the thirteenth century, its statues once brilliantly coloured and backed by gilded niches.

The central tower was built in the twelfth century as far as the stringcourse and its upper portion added in 1321. The south-west tower dates from 1386 and the north-west from 1424. The north porch was built in the late twelfth century.

INTERIOR

The building of Bishop de Bohun's church to whose design the present building owes its unity of form, began in 1186 with the western bays of the choir and the eastern bays of the nave. The western bays of the nave were not completed until 1239. The sculpture of the capitals of the northern arcade is noteworthy. The font survives from the earlier, twelfth-century building, and there is a seventeenth-century lectern and a sixteenth-century pulpit adjacent to the western pillars of the crossing, the eastern piers flanking the thirteenth-century pulpitum. The great scissor arches, added in 1360 to receive the weight of the heightened tower, are a unique feature. The rood is a modern replacement of that which occupied the same place before the Reformation.

Both transepts were built at the close of the twelfth century. On the north side the beautiful stairway, worn by many feet since its building in 1360, and having a delicately sculptured corbel, leads now to the Chain Gate and the Chapter House.

A double-arched doorway gives access to the Chapter House, where the wall seating has finely sculptured canopies and a slender pillar upholds a roof of delicate workmanship. Stairway, Chapter House and undercroft beneath were added in 1263. The undercroft retains the medieval ironwork of its door and a pyx canopy which once hung before the high altar.

The Lady Chapel was added at the eastern extension early in the fourteenth century, replacing an earlier chapel to the south, joined to the choir by the retrochoir of 1360.

There are four chantry chapels of the fifteenth century, that of Bishop Beckington in the south choir aisle retaining its medieval colouring. An alabaster tomb in the Chapel of St. Calixtus bears delicate figures.

The cloisters were largely rebuilt in 1457, with a library above one of its walks and a singing-room above another.

The clock in the north transept, famous for its jousting

knights and the figure of Jack Blandifer, was made in the fourteenth century.

Unique among cathedrals, Wells retains its medieval houses once provided for the vicars-choral, together with their chapel and dining-hall. The Chain Gate was added in the fourteenth century to permit them to gain access, dry-shod, to the church.

WINCHESTER

A church was erected here in 645 and enlarged in the tenth century. It was rebuilt between 1079 and 1093 and attained the grandeur of its present form between 1346 and 1404 when William of Wykeham was bishop.

At one time the capital of England, Winchester saw the coronation both of the Confessor and of Cœur de Lion, and the marriage of Mary.

EXTERIOR

The Norman central tower collapsed in 1107, supposedly in protest at the burial of the evil Rufus beneath it, and was rebuilt later in the same century.

The west front is fourteenth century.

The north transept has a walled-up doorway which once admitted pilgrims to St. Swithin's shrine. Adjacent to the south transept are the remains of the Chapter House which was demolished in the seventeenth century.

INTERIOR

The great fourteenth-century west window contains fragments of seventeenth-century glass. The bronze statues of James I and Charles I once ornamented the screen.

The nave is fourteenth century. The striking font is two hundred years older and sculptured with scenes from the story of St. Nicholas, patron saint of children. In contrast the transepts have survived from the eleventh-century church.

Adjoining the north transept is the Chapel of the Holy Sepulchre, with medieval mural paintings on its walls.

The choir is early fourteenth century, completed before the erection of the nave, and flanked by sixteenth-century screens on which rest mortuary chests containing the bones of Saxon kings. The high altar has a fifteenth-century reredos-screen, the statues recently restored, the original figures having been destroyed at the Reformation. The magnificent choir stalls were carved in 1308, the pulpit in the fifteenth century. The beautiful, but damaged, sculpture of the Madonna is fourteenth century.

The shrine of Bishop Swithin, who died in 862, once stood beyond the altar, attracting great numbers of pilgrims. He had left instructions that he was to be buried outside the church and when his body was transferred to the interior in 971 it is reputed to have rained for forty days in protest:

> If on St. Swithin's feast the wellkin lowers,
> And every penthouse streams with hasty showers,
> Twice twenty days shall clouds their fleeces drain
> And wash the pavement with incessant rain.

The roof of the presbytery is ornamented with bosses carved in the sixteenth century. Beyond it, the early twelfth-century Lady Chapel was extended by Henry VII in commemoration of Prince Arthur's baptism. The murals were painted in 1500.

No other cathedral possesses so rich a collection of chantry chapels. North and south of the high altar are those of Bishop Gardiner, 1555, and Bishop Fox, 1528, the latter with cadaver and handsome roof bosses. North and south of the Lady Chapel are the chantries of Bishop Wayneflete, 1486, and Cardinal Beaufort, 1447, looked down upon by a modern effigy of Joan of Arc whom he condemned to burning. East of this is the chantry of Bishop Langton, 1501.

In the south transept are the oldest wrought-iron gates

in the country. The Izaak Walton window is in the Chapel of Prior Silkestede.

The south aisle of the nave has the Chantry of Bishop Edington, with alabaster effigy, and that of William of Wykeham, three little clerks praying at his feet.

The crypt is eleventh century.

WORCESTER

There was a bishopric here in the seventh century and it is reputed that Oswald, who was bishop from 983, built a cathedral with twenty-eight altars. The Confessor elected Wulfstan to the see on Oswald's death. He was the only bishop to retain his cathedra after the Conquest, and assisted at the coronation of the Conqueror. Oswald's cathedral had been burned by the Danes in 1041 and had since remained in a state of ruin. Wulfstan now began a new building. Fires did much damage in 1113 and 1202. After the battle of Worcester Cromwell's army used the church as a prison and was responsible for considerable vandalism. In the last century extensive restoration was carried out.

EXTERIOR

The central tower of the Norman church collapsed in 1175, and the present majestic tower was erected in 1370.

The spacious north porch is of the late fourteenth century, subsequently restored.

INTERIOR

The west window is of the nineteenth century. The cathedral retains little medieval stained glass, most of this having been destroyed at the time of the Reformation and again during the Civil War.

The two western bays of the northern arcade belong to the building of 1170 and have richly decorated triforiums. The remaining western bays, together with the Jesus Chapel and the south arcade, date from 1370.

The north aisle contains a pleasant memorial of the early seventeenth century and the richly sculptured Beaucham tomb, where the effigies have swans for pillows.

The tower is supported by somewhat unsightly cross ribs at the level of triforium and clerestory.

The north transept retains a Romanesque doorway from Wulfstan's church and contains a memorial by Roubilliac of the eighteenth century.

The choir was rebuilt in the thirteenth century. The screen was removed at the Reformation, but a number of medieval misericords remain. The high altar has an ornate and heavily sculptured Victorian reredos.

In front of the altar is the fifteenth-century tomb of King John with effigy of 1232. Once it was flanked by the shrines of Oswald and Wulfstan, but these have entirely disappeared and are remembered only by the small figures either side of the king's head. The grave was opened last century and the skeleton, 5 ft. 5 in. in height, found lying intact in its robes; the fragments of a monk's cowl were also found, supporting the report that the king was buried in a cowl at his request, hoping thereby to obtain entry into heaven.

South of the altar is the beautifully sculptured chantry of Prince Arthur, son of Henry VII, who died at the age of fifteen in 1502.

The Lady Chapel, skilfully rebuilt last century, has a noble east window of 1224, a richly decorated vault and un-remarkable stained glass. The sculptured scenes at the east end are a feature, and the sacrist's window from which watch was kept on the shrines is unique.

The crypt belonged to Wulfstan's church and, though partially filled now by blocks and rubble to provide support for the fourteenth-century building, the forest of simple Romanesque columns is attractive. The crypt once held the shrine of St. Oswald.

The cloisters were rebuilt in 1380, retaining portions of the Norman cloisters. The unadorned lavatorium survives; the piercing of the piers is an unusual feature. The south walk has bosses forming a jesse tree. A passageway, with simple arcading, remains from Wulfstan's time.

The Chapter House was erected in 1140, but windows and doorway are fifteenth century. The fourteenth-century refectory, with Norman doorway, has been restored and is used by the cathedral school. Only ruins remain of the other domestic buildings of the monastery, dorter and guest-house, but the sturdy fortified gateway of 1350, with its original doors, has been restored.

YORK

Augustine converted Ethelbert, king of Kent, to the Christian faith at the close of the sixth century. In the following century his daughter Ethelburga married Edwin of Northumberland and took her chaplain Paulinus with her. Paulinus baptized Edwin at York in 627, a wooden church being erected for the ceremony, and this was the beginning of York Minster.

The wooden church was replaced by one of stone which was probably destroyed during the Conqueror's ravaging of the north. At the end of the eleventh century it was rebuilt by the Norman archbishop, but within forty years was so damaged by fire as to become ruinous. After a lapse of time it was again rebuilt at the end of that century. The present church dates, for the most part, from the thirteenth to the fifteenth centuries. Two more recent fires, in 1829 and 1840, damaged the fabric.

It is the largest of the English cathedrals and has always been in the charge of secular canons.

EXTERIOR

The great central tower was raised in 1480. The south-west tower was built in 1456, the north-west eighteen years later.

The west front was erected between 1317 and 1340. The western doors are nineteenth century.

North of the church is a thirteenth-century chapel now in use as a library.

INTERIOR

The nave was built between 1291 and 1338 and retains its fourteenth-century wooden roof. The west window dates from 1338, and the west wall is sculptured with scenes from the story of Samson.

The splendid pulpitum was made between 1475 and 1500, and its statues have been restored. There are eighteenth-century wrought-iron gates to the choir and the vaulting of the entrance arch has a delicately sculptured medallion of the Blessed Virgin.

The pulpit west of the pulpitum is of the present century, the lectern seventeenth century.

The north transept was built in 1251 and in it is the Five Sisters' window with grisaille glass. The ceiling has fifteenth-century bosses, but is otherwise a modern restoration.

The minster retains a greater quantity of ancient stained glass than any other cathedral. On the north side of the nave a twelfth-century panel may be the oldest surviving stained glass in the country.

A vestibule joins the north transept to the Chapter House, built 1286 to 1340, with medieval ironwork on its doors and stalls and handsome canopies circling its walls. Its immense wooden roof, 58 ft. in width, unsupported by any central column, ranks among the great engineering achievements of medieval times. The windows contain glass of the thirteenth, fourteenth and sixteenth centuries. The Horn of Ulf, reputedly presented to the minster in the time of Canute, is kept here.

The choir, which stands at an angle to the nave, was built between 1361 and 1425, its eastern window having early fifteenth-century glass. The stalls replace those burned in the fire of 1829.

North-east of the high altar is the tomb of Archbishop Scrope, beheaded in 1405, who is also commemorated in a stained-glass window. Another window commemorates St. William, a twelfth-century archbishop revered as a saint whose shrine once stood east of the altar.

The Lady Chapel was added in 1425. On its northern side the Chapel of St. Stephen retains what was originally the high altar, with a delicate terra-cotta panel of the crucifixion for reredos.

The south transept, in which is a blocked Norman arch, gives access to the fourteenth-century Zouche Chapel, which contains the only two medieval choir stalls to survive the fire.

There are relics of the earlier churches in the crypt, the eastern columns belonging to the eleventh-century church and those to the west, with more ornate capitals, of the late twelfth century. A beautifully sculptured but damaged panel of the Blessed Virgin belonged to the Romanesque church, and a dried-up and blocked well may mark the place of Edwin's baptism which is commemorated by the splendid font cover by Sir Ninian Comper. At a lower level may be seen the base of a Roman column of 306.

XIV. THE CHURCHES OF SCOTLAND AND WALES

The Episcopal Church of Scotland was founded by Celtic monks and developed as an independent, national Church acknowledging the authority neither of Canterbury nor—except for spasmodic periods—of Rome. Like its sister Church in England, it suffered drastic reforms in the sixteenth century and persecution during the Commonwealth. It was disestablished and disendowed in the eighteenth century on account of its persistent loyalty to the House of Stuart. Its buildings were given to the Presbyterians who, having no bishops, either converted the cathedrals into parish churches or allowed them to fall into disrepair.

It was not until the end of the century that the repeal of the penal laws permitted the impoverished Church, its ministry now reduced to two bishops and forty priests, to provide itself with new church buildings. As of old, the Episcopal Church of Scotland today is a self-governing and national Church forming, like the Churches of England, Wales and America, an independent province of the worldwide Anglican Communion.

The Christian faith was planted in England during the Roman occupation, but failed to survive the withdrawal of the legions and the invasions of heathen Scandinavians in the fifth century. The Christians fled to Wales where, in the sixth century, missionary monks in close contact with the Irish Church preserved and propagated the faith.

In 596 the Roman mission, led by Augustine, landed in Kent. Later Augustine held two conferences with the British bishops on the banks of the Severn, demanding that they accept him as their archbishop, but his proud and pompous manner led them to reject him.

It was not until Norman times that the Church of Wales was united to the Church of England and so remained until the present century. In 1920 the Church in Wales was disestablished and disendowed, so that once again it is a self-governing and national Church forming an independent province of the Anglican Communion.

SCOTLAND

ABERDEEN,
   St. Andrew's: New Foundation
   St. Machair's: Secular Canons
BRECHIN: Secular Canons
DORNOCH: Secular Canons
DUNBLANE: Secular Canons
DUNDEE: New Foundation
DUNKELD: Secular Canons
EDINBURGH,
   St. Giles: Secular Canons
   St. Mary's: New Foundation

ELGIN: Secular Canons
FORTROSE: Secular Canons
GLASGOW,
   St. Mary's: New Foundation
   St. Mungo's: Secular Canons
INVERNESS: New Foundation
IONA: Benedictine Monastery
KIRKWALL: Secular Canons
OBAN: New Foundation
PERTH: New Foundation
ST. ANDREWS: Augustinian Canons

WALES

BANGOR: Secular Canons
BRECON: Priory Church
LLANDAFF: Secular Canons

NEWPORT: Parish Church
ST. ASAPH: Secular Canons
ST. DAVID'S: Secular Canons

XV. THE SCOTTISH CATHEDRALS

ABERDEEN: St. Andrew's

The cathedral, dedicated to St. Andrew, is notable as the descendant of the chapel in Bishop Skinner's house where in

1784 Bishop Seabury was consecrated as first bishop of the American Episcopal Church. Bishop Skinner's private chapel then served the small congregation of penalized Episcopalians in Aberdeen until the erection of a separate chapel on adjoining ground in 1792 and, in the following century, the present church.

The nineteenth-century nave is by Arnold Simpson. Chancel and sanctuary were rebuilt in the present century. The foundation stone, laid by Joseph Kennedy when American Ambassador to Britain, is north of the high altar which is beneath a handsome baldacchino. The west window, designed by Sir Ninian Comper, commemorates the centenary of Bishop Seabury's consecration.

The roof of the north aisle, which terminates in Sir Robert Lorimer's Lady Chapel, is decorated with the arms of the forty-eight American States. The statue of the Virgin is by Maxine Duff.

The south aisle ends in the Suther Chapel of the Reserved Sacrament and is entered through a finely decorated screen. The roof is decorated with the heraldic arms of the forty-eight families of North-east Scotland who remained loyal to the Church throughout its persecution. There is a statue of Bishop Skinner by Flaxman and memorials of the eighteenth-century congregation.

ABERDEEN: St. Machair's

St. Machair was a disciple of St. Columba sent from Iona to convert the northern Picts. The ex-cathedral, now a parish kirk, stands on the site chosen by the saint for his church, but contains no work earlier than the fourteenth century, though the present building was founded in 1136. It is the only granite cathedral in Britain.

Only nave and aisles survive. The central tower, built in 1500, fell in 1688, destroying the transepts. The fine west front is flanked by sandstone 'broach' steeples added in the sixteenth century, and the round doorway has a vesica between its twin, pointed entrances.

The nave is fifteenth century with handsome sixteenth-century roof. The south transept, in ruinous condition, shelters an episcopal tomb of the sixteenth century. The east window contains notable glass and the window of the south aisle tells the story of the patron saint.

BRECHIN

The ex-cathedral stands on the site of a Culdee abbey and retains portions of the fabric of the twelfth-century church founded by David I. The transepts were destroyed in 1807, but have since been restored. The fine choir, with restored roof, is thirteenth century and the tower fourteenth century. The porch and the west window are noteworthy. The choir is in use as a parish church.

DORNOCH

The ex-cathedral, its low tower crowned by a short spire, is thirteenth century, but was much damaged by the Reformers and later by tasteless restoration. The west window is noteworthy.

DUNBLANE

The ex-cathedral was founded by David I on the site of a sixth-century church.

The tower has its Norman lower story, but the upper story is fifteenth century. The west front is thirteenth century with notable doorway and lancet windows.

The great nave has a double-mullioned clerestory, restored and re-roofed in last century. The choir, restored in the present century, is in use as a parish church. The absence of transepts is an unusual feature.

I

The south aisle has a vaulted chamber which may have been a prison for witches. It shelters fifteenth-century stalls and the effigy of the bishop who crowned James II in 1437. In the north aisle is a Celtic stone of A.D. 900 and a thirteenth-century effigy. The modern pulpit has figures illustrative of the church's history.

Some ruins of the bishop's palace may still be seen.

DUNDEE

The cathedral, built in the Gothic style, was designed by Sir George Gilbert Scott and consecrated in 1855, becoming in 1904 the cathedral of the diocese previously served by the cathedral at Brechin.

The nave has arcades of slender columns bearing pointed arches. The apsidal chancel has a reredos of Italian mosaics above its high altar and choir stalls bearing the figures of St. Andrew, King David I, St. Margaret of Scotland, and Modwenna, abbess of a local religious house. A brass in the centre of the choir marks the grave of the founder-bishop. The north transept has an altar and reredos from a former mission church and the Lady Chapel reredos depicts the Annunciation. The font stands on a pedestal which once belonged to Lindores Abbey and a cabinet has carved panels from the abbey's choir stalls. The cathedral is dedicated to St. Paul.

DUNKELD

The ex-cathedral, occupying a picturesque site, was wrecked by the sixteenth-century reformers, but partially restored by the Dukes of Atholl in the following century. The roofless nave, used as a burial ground, is fifteenth century, and the choir, now restored as a parish church, a century earlier. The tower is late fifteenth century. The aisle windows display flamboyant tracery; the west window is not centrally placed. In the former Chapter House are the tombs of the Dukes of Atholl. There is a fourteenth-century effigy of a bishop and the effigy of the Wolf of Badenoch, brother of Richard III.

EDINBURGH: St. Giles

St. Giles, now the principal Presbyterian church of the city, served only briefly as a cathedral during the seventeenth century. Occupying the site of a Norman church destroyed in 1385, the present building has been so drastically restored that little of its ancient character remains. Prior to the ministry of John Knox in the sixteenth century forty-four altars are said to have been demolished. In the last century the church was partitioned into three churches.

Both choir and nave have double aisles, and the former retains its vaulted roof. An unusual feature is that the choir is of greater length than the nave. The fifteenth-century tower is the church's most notable feature, with flying buttresses supporting a crown and miniature steeple. There are a number of interesting memorials and Sir Robert Lorimer's handsome and ornate Chapel of the Thistle, added in 1911, has good heraldic glass. The modern bronze statue of Knox is noteworthy.

EDINBURGH: St. Mary's

The diocese was founded by Charles I with St. Giles as its cathedral, but this arrangement lasted only a short time. After the repeal of the Penal Laws St. Paul's Church became the pro-cathedral in 1874 until the present cathedral was consecrated in 1879. It was designed in the Gothic style by Sir George Gilbert Scott. The central spire and those flanking the western façade were completed in this century. The rood was designed by Sir Robert Lorimer. The north transept is the baptistry, the south a War Memorial chapel;

a further chapel is dedicated to King Charles and All Souls. The clerestory windows display the armorial bearings of noble Scottish families.

ELGIN

The ex-cathedral, now ruinous, represents some of the finest architecture in Scotland. Known as the 'Lanthorne of the North', it was condemned by the reformers as a 'Romish Vanity', stripped of its roof, its interior wrecked and its great rood screen wantonly destroyed. Built in the thirteenth century, it was badly damaged by fire in the same century and again in the following century when the Wolf of Badenoch destroyed it. The rebuilt central tower collapsed in 1538 and again in the eighteenth century.

The west front has a richly decorated doorway with sculptured tympanum; above the fifteenth-century traceried rose window are carved the arms of Scotland. The buttressed, octagonal towers are fourteenth century, and have pinnacles enriched with arcaded niches. The façade and doorway of the south transept are also noteworthy fourteenth-century work as is the traceried window in the south wall.

The nave, with double aisles, is now marked only by the bases of its columns. Choir and raised chancel retain their lancet windows of the clerestory; the lancets of the eastern wall have piers in place of mullions.

In the choir a stone marks the grave of the founder-bishop, and a Saxon sculptured stone is to be noted.

The groined roof of the fifteenth-century Chapter House is supported by a central pier, but the windows are of later date. A small lavatorium has a piscena in which, in 1748, a widow cradled her infant son who later gained fame as General Anderson. A portion of the sixteenth-century episcopal palace remains. Some of the stones in the churchyard bear quaint inscriptions.

FORTROSE

The cathedral, built of red sandstone in the thirteenth and fourteenth centuries, is now ruinous, though the fourteenth-century south aisle retains its vault. The undercroft of the thirteenth-century Chapter House is used as a courtroom.

GLASGOW: St. Mary the Virgin

Dedicated to St. Mary, with a side chapel to St. Anne, the cathedral perpetuates the dedication of the late medieval church at the Tron, which was second in importance to St. Mungo's Cathedral in the latter part of the sixteenth century and the seventeenth century. Episcopalian worship appears to have ceased in the early building after 1688, and it was not till 1825 that another episcopalian church in the city adopted the name of St. Mary's. This congregation moved west to the present site in 1871, and their church was established as the cathedral of the diocese in 1908.

Designed by Sir George Gilbert Scott, the church was built between 1870 and 1884. Its style is Early English, with suggestions of Early Decorated, but does not show any of the characteristics of the architect.

The attractive spire to the design of John Oldred Scott was completed in 1893. It contains the only peal of bells in the city. The base of the tower is ornamented with the statues of four bishops of Glasgow: Bishop Jocelyn, who initiated the building of St. Mungo's Cathedral in the twelfth century; Bishop Turnbull, who founded the university in the fourteenth century; Archbishop Leighton, the saintly scholar of the seventeenth century, who tried to act as religious peacemaker; and the nineteenth-century Bishop Trower, who bears on his arm a model of the new cathedral.

The interior is simple, with open timber roof beams, which form a wooden groin vault at the crossing. The corbel stone in the nave portray eight British or national patron saints, including St. Margaret and St. Andrew, a motif echoed in the Celtic saints depicted on the reredos behind the High Altar.

As well as the chapel of St. Anne, to the north of the high altar, there are two recently created transept chapels. The southern, St. Saviour's, again bears the name of an earlier Glasgow church. The northern is a requiem chapel.

GLASGOW: St. Mungo's

St. Kentigern, who died in 603, worked as a pioneer missionary in Strathclyde, where he was known affectionately as 'Mungo, the dear one'. The cathedral, best-preserved of the medieval cathedrals of Scotland, was raised above his grave, replacing an earlier church. The base of his shrine is still to be seen in the crypt. The choir is now in use as a parish church. In the sixteenth century the building was divided into three churches.

The thirteenth-century central tower has a spire added in the early fifteenth century. Two western towers have been demolished.

The aisled nave, with triforium and clerestory, is four-teenth century, well proportioned, the columns with un-adorned capitals and a handsome, fourteenth-century roof. The transepts are unusual, having no projection.

The choir, closed by a fifteenth-century pulpitum depict-ing the seven deadly sins, is of splendid thirteenth-century workmanship, with square-ended ambulatory for use by pilgrims visiting the saint's shrine. Eastwards are four chapels, with lancet windows, separated by shafts supporting a vaulted roof. Below the choir is a crypt which, owing to the fall of the site, is on ground level. Here the chapels are repeated, but separated by solid walls. This crypt was the first portion of the church to be consecrated in 1197, but few remnants of earliest building remain, the present aisled crypt with its fine vaulting being early thirteenth century.

North of the choir is a square sacristy, the central pillar

displaying the arms of the founder-bishop, below which is the early fifteenth-century Chapter House reached by a turret stairway. The entrance is richly carved, and a tombstone of nine martyred Covenanters bears a quaint inscription.

A second crypt, known as Blackader's after its founder-bishop, lies south of the crossing, intended possibly to support a transept which was never built. In the early fifteenth-century vaulted roof is depicted the two-wheeled cart on which St. Kentigern is said to have brought the body of St. Fergus to Glasgow.

The stained glass is modern and unremarkable.

INVERNESS: St. Andrew's

Erected in 1866 to the design of Dr. Alexander Ross, this was the first cathedral built in Britain after the Reformation. The west end is flanked by two massive towers of rose-coloured stone and over the entrance is sculptured Christ blessing his Apostles. Consisting of nave, transepts and apsidal chancel, the nave arches are upheld by pillars of polished granite; a finely carved oaken screen separates nave from chancel. The baptistry beneath the south tower has a life-size angel font copied from Thorvaldsen's font in Copenhagen. There is a fifteenth-century panel by Sano di Pietro depicting the Virgin and Child with Franciscan saints, and five icons presented by a Czar of Russia.

IONA: St. Mary's

In 563 St. Columba came with twelve companions from Ireland to the Island of Iona as an act of repentance for the deaths of two thousand people in a battle fought on his behalf. His monastery of beehive cells formed a missionary centre for the conversion of the Picts.

The ex-cathedral, much restored, was built in the thirteenth century. Its squat tower rests on Norman arches and has traceried windows of later date. Five round-headed windows are above the pointed doorway of the west end and the sacristy has an elaborately carved doorway of 1500. The Chapter House, with Scriptorium above, has a thirteenth-century doorway and the capitals of the nave arcade are noteworthy. In the chancel are the tombs of two abbots of the early sixteenth century and a fourteenth-century sedilia. A polished stone kept behind a grill is said to be St. Columba's pillow.

KIRKWALL

The cruciform ex-cathedral is dedicated to St. Magnus, who was murdered in 1115, the church raised in 1137 by Rognvald Jarl III, nephew of the murderer. In 1926 the remains of both the saint and the founder were found secreted in the fabric. The building is now used as a parish church.

The tower was built in 1525 on Early English arches. The spire was destroyed by lightning in 1671.

The nave, narrow in proportion to its height, was probably built by the same masons who raised Durham Cathedral. The round arches are upheld by huge stone columns with undecorated capitals. The thirteenth-century choir ends in an east wall pierced by four lancets and a rose window inserted in 1511. Clerestory and vault are also thirteenth century. The south aisle has a sixteenth-century crocketted tomb. There are some remains of the episcopal palace where King Haakon of Norway died in 1263 after ceding the Hebrides to Scotland.

OBAN

The cathedral of St. John consists of two buildings joined, but without harmony. The nave of grey stone is the first parish church consecrated in 1864. The sanctuary, choir, chapel, sacristy and aisle, of red stone, were built in 1908 to the design of James Chalmers, portions of an uncompleted scheme for an entirely new cathedral. A tower above the entrance at the south-east was intended, but never realized. The foundations proved unable to bear the weight of the central tower at the crossing which had belonged to Chalmers' original design. The united buildings were opened for use in 1910 and given cathedral status in 1928, the crossing now lit by a lantern added in 1958.

It is intended that the cathedral shall eventually be designed in the form of a Greek cross, the altar at the centre beneath the lantern and the upper walls of the old church demolished to allow for a new arm forming the nave. Screens will permit portions of the building to be shut off during the winter when, owing to the absence of visitors, congregations are smaller.

Considerable renovation and improvement were carried out in 1968.

PERTH

The cathedral, to the design of a Mr. Butterfield, was partially completed and opened for worship in 1850, serving the united dioceses of St. Andrews, Dunkeld and Dunblane. It is dedicated to St. Ninian, the son of a British chieftain who, at the end of the fifth century, worked as a pioneer missionary among the Picts of southern Scotland. The building was not completed until the present century.

The lofty nave and chancel are in the Gothic style separated by a stone screen bearing a rood, designed by Sir Ninian Comper. The clerestory windows contain the arms of benefactors. The reredos of the high altar and double sedilia are made in Aberfeldy stone, the baldacchino of Cornish granite. The Founders' Window depicts the story of the patron saint. In the sanctuary is the tomb and bronze effigy of Bishop Torrey, who was Primus at the beginning of the present century and responsible for the enlargement of the cathedral.

I*

ST. ANDREWS

The sole remnants of the first cathedral are the tall, square tower of St. Rule's built in 1080, and remains of the narrow, apsidal choir of later date.

The second cathedral, dedicated to St. Andrew, was built by Augustinian Canons in 1160 although it had to wait 150 years for consecration. Once the largest cathedral in Scotland, only the ruins of east and west ends remain, the latter with recessed doorway and buttressed turret; the turreted eastern wall of the Lady Chapel was built in 1202. The nave of fourteen bays was damaged by fire in 1378, and neglect and the elements completed its destruction. The arcaded wall of the Chapter House also remains.

St. Andrew, our Lord's disciple, is said to have been martyred on a diagonal cross at Patras in Greece. In the fourth century the Emperor Constantius came with an army to seize his relics, but, warned by an angel, St. Rule or Regulus rescued them and after four years of wandering was shipwrecked in Scotland where the relics afterwards remained. The Romanesque tower of St. Rule may have been built to guard these or other relics. A sarcophagus of A.D. 900 is to be seen there.

XVI. THE WELSH CATHEDRALS

BANGOR

Soon after the withdrawal of the Roman legions Britain was invaded by heathen hordes from the North and there was a large-scale emigration to the comparative safety of Wales and Cornwall. During the sixth century there was a vigorous Christian movement in Wales led by monks who were in close touch with the Irish Church. Among these missionaries was Deiniol, who built a church at Bangor in 525, probably a simple construction of wattle work surrounded by the beehive cells of his monks. In 545 Deiniol was made bishop, so his church then became his cathedral. Bangor Cathedral, on the site of Deiniol's church, thus probably occupies the most ancient cathedral site in the British Isles.

Deiniol's church was destroyed by the Normans, who despised the simplicity of the Celtic monks, in 1071, and replaced by a small, aisleless church which in turn was destroyed in the thirteenth century and its successor in the fifteenth century.

The present cathedral is therefore heir to a turbulent but ancient history. Erected in the sixteenth century, tower and transepts were rebuilt last century by Gilbert Scott.

The tower is sixteenth century. A blocked window and a buttress in the south wall of the chancel are the sole remnants of Norman work.

The cathedral shelters the plain, twelfth-century tomb of a local prince, Owain Gwynedd, and a medieval carved figure of our Lord known as the Mostyn Christ. Other treasures are a charter of the time of Elizabeth I and a finely preserved Pontifical of Bishop Anian, who baptized Edward II.

BRECON

Originally a church served by Benedictine monks, this became a cathedral in 1923.

The tower is thirteenth century. The severely designed nave is fourteenth century. The rood screen, dividing nave and chancel, has gone, but its supports and the doors which gave access to the loft are preserved. The choir contains fine thirteenth-century work, with five lancets above the high altar. On the north is the Chapel of St. Keyne, perhaps the most interesting part of the building, with barrel roof and fourteenth-century effigy, dedicated originally to the patron saints of shoemakers, SS. Crispin and Crispinian. The north transept has triple lancets and a squint; it now shelters a military chapel. The thirteenth-century south transept has two bays and the restored Chapel of St. Lawrence. The font is Norman.

LLANDAFF

The name means Place by the (River) Taff. Teilo, a missionary bishop of the sixth century, founded a monastery here, with a school, leading a rigorous religious order known as the Watermen. He was related to St. David and was accompanied by his cousin Dubricius or Dyfrig, who shares with him credit for founding the first church here. Dubricius later retired to Bardsey Island where he lived as a hermit. His bones were brought back to the cathedral in 1120. Until 1840 the offices of Bishop and Dean were united.

The building suffered considerable damage from a land mine in the last war, far exceeding that inflicted upon it in previous centuries by Reformers, Cromwellians, and the tasteless restoration work of the seventeenth century.

The western front is thirteenth century and has figures of Christ the King and St. Teilo. The pinnacles of the fifteenth-century north tower were blown down in a storm in

1703, doing much damage, and the south tower fell before a second storm twenty years later, to be restored in the last century. Along the south wall of the nave and continuing on the north wall are the sculptured heads of British sovereigns, and in the Lady Chapel medieval gargoyles.

The detached Norman belfry, ruinous since the fifteenth century, may be seen near the Deanery, and the ruined gateway which once gave access to the episcopal palace now serves as entrance to the school.

North and south entrances are twelfth century, as is the nave. The clerestory was rebuilt on the medieval pattern in the last century. The attractive modern font is by Alan Durst. In the north bay adjacent to the choir is an alabaster tomb of the fifteenth century. Here should be noted the sub-arch on the south side intended to support a central tower which was never built.

The church is dominated by Epstein's impressive Majesta set against the concrete organ case supported by light concrete arches designed by George Pace, marking the division between nave and choir. Pre-Raphaelite figures from the choir stalls decorate the case.

The Illtyd Chapel beneath the north-west tower has a Rossetti triptych above its altar, and at the eastern extremity of the north aisle in the St. Dyfrig Chapel are six charming della robbia panels designed by Burne-Jones.

St. Teilo's thirteenth-century shrine is south of the high altar, the altar framed by a Romanesque arch. Beyond it, in the Lady Chapel, are a Madonna and Child by A. G. Walker, stained glass by Christopher Webb and a reredos of bronze panels depicting wild flowers.

A Celtic cross is displayed in the south aisle, near the entrance to the small, two-story Chapter House with its charming, modern pepper-pot roof appropriately crowning the thirteenth-century masonry, a gilded Angel Gabriel on its summit.

A military chapel dedicated to St. David has been added

on the north-west with a processional way guarded within by medieval gargoyles.

NEWPORT

The church served the local parish until made the pro-cathedral of the diocese of Monmouth in 1921 and in 1949 the cathedral. Dedicated to St. Woolos, the name is a corruption of Gwynllyw, who was converted to the faith in the sixth century and built here a church as an act of penitence for his past life. In Norman times the appointment of the vicar was by the Benedictine monks of Gloucester, passing at the Reformation to the bishop. The first Norman church was burned in 1462.

The tower is fifteenth century, the second story being added at the end of the century and the uppermost story in the following century.

The Norman builders apparently preserved the Saxon church, building on to its eastern wall, thus providing a chapel between tower and nave, the present fabric dating from the thirteenth century. Of the windows, however, only the octagonal one in the south wall is original.

The magnificent arch leading to the nave is Norman as are the arcades of the nave, with chamfered capitals, and the clerestory with its splayed windows. The window on the south side is thirteenth century. The aisles, rebuilt in the Perpendicular style, are of the fifteenth century.

The chancel was restored in the last century and extended in the present century. The rose window above the altar has glass by John Piper.

ST. ASAPH

About 560 St. Kentigern, the pioneer missionary to southern Scotland, was exiled from Strathclyde and founded a monastery in this district where St. Asaph succeeded him as bishop. The church, rebuilt by the Normans, was destroyed in the thirteenth century by the English and in the following century by Glyndwr. The building suffered during the time of Cromwell and in 1714 as the result of a storm which stripped the roof. In 1779 the Chapter House was demolished and the building left in a ruinous condition. Restoration was undertaken by Gilbert Scott at the end of the last century.

The central tower is much restored.

A memorial in the churchyard commemorates those who translated the Bible and Prayer-Book into Welsh in the sixteenth century.

The nave pillars are without capitals. The clerestory dates from 1403. The stalls are fifteenth-century workmanship.

The Lady Chapel was refurnished in 1960.

There is an effigy of Bishop Anian II, who rebuilt the church in the thirteenth century, and a seventeenth-century Spanish Madonna. The library includes among its possessions a New Testament of 1567 in Welsh, and other rare books.

ST. DAVID'S

Dewi Sant, St. David, founded a monastery here in the sixth century. The Normans gave the church into the charge of canons, consecrating their first cathedral building in 1131. The fabric was tastelessly restored by John Nash at the close of the eighteenth century and, with better result, by Sir Gilbert Scott a hundred years later.

The cathedral is approached through one of the four gateways which, in the fourteenth century, gave access to the precincts. A thirteenth-century octagonal tower, built to hold a ring of bells, received its bells only in the present century. The tower collapsed in 1220 and only its lowest stage remains, the second stage being built in the fourteenth and the uppermost stage in the sixteenth century. The original bell frame is preserved within it. The tower indicates the pitch of the original nave roof before this was lowered. In the east gable of the Lady Chapel a fourteenth-century niche holds a Madonna and Child.

The twelfth-century nave is notable for its unusual round arches. The windows have fourteenth-century tracery, and the roof is sixteenth century.

In the handsome fourteenth-century pulpitum, on the south side, is the tomb of its builder, Bishop Gower. The statue of the patron saint is modern. The choir below the crossing is enclosed by a screen beyond the pulpitum, and has fifteenth-century canopied stalls with interesting misereres. The depleted shrine of St. David stands north of the presbytery. Cathedra, with chaplains' seats, and wooden sedilia of beautiful Perpendicular design are of early sixteenth-century workmanship. The high altar is backed by three windows now filled with mosaics. Before it stands the tomb of Edmund Tudor, grandfather of Henry VIII, brought here from the Grey Friars' church at Carmarthen at the time of the dissolution of the monasteries. Below the central window a narrow opening once provided pilgrims with a view of the saint's shrine.

In the north transept the restored Chapel of St. Thomas, set at an angle and erected in the thirteenth century, has its original double piscena. Above are two stories approached by a spiral staircase, used respectively as Chapter House and treasury. At the termination of the north choir aisle is the fourteenth-century chantry chapel of St. Nicholas, with a second chantry chapel dedicated to St. Edward terminating the south aisle and, between them, the rebuilt fourteenth-century Lady Chapel with roof restored at the beginning of the present century.

West of the Lady Chapel the ambulatory once formed the eastern boundary of a rectangular space open to the sky. In the sixteenth century this space was made the Trinity Chapel, with fine fan-vaulting. Here now rest in a casket the relics of St. David discovered, secreted in the fabric, in the last century. The recess which they occupy originally provided the pilgrims' view of the shrine standing in the presbytery. An eleventh-century tombstone is seen in the south transept. The south porch was added in the fourteenth century.

The sole relic of the fourteenth-century college of the vicars-choral is the chapel of St. Mary's north of the cathedral and now restored for use as a hall.

INDEX OF PLACE-NAMES